LAYERS OF LEARNING

YEAR FOUR • UNIT ONE

AMERICAN GOVERNMENT
U.S.A.
HEAT & TEMPERATURE
PATRIOTIC MUSIC

Published by HooDoo Publishing
United States of America
© 2016 Layers of Learning
ISBN 978-1534719668

Units at a Glance: Topics For All Four Years of the Layers of Learning Program

1	History	Geography	Science	The Arts
1	Mesopotamia	Maps & Globes	Planets	Cave Paintings
2	Egypt	Map Keys	Stars	Egyptian Art
3	Europe	Global Grids	Earth & Moon	Crafts
4	Ancient Greece	Wonders	Satellites	Greek Art
5	Babylon	Mapping People	Humans in Space	Poetry
6	The Levant	Physical Earth	Laws of Motion	List Poems
7	Phoenicians	Oceans	Motion	Moral Stories
8	Assyrians	Deserts	Fluids	Rhythm
9	Persians	Arctic	Waves	Melody
10	Ancient China	Forests	Machines	Chinese Art
11	Early Japan	Mountains	States of Matter	Line & Shape
12	Arabia	Rivers & Lakes	Atoms	Color & Value
13	Ancient India	Grasslands	Elements	Texture & Form
14	Ancient Africa	Africa	Bonding	African Tales
15	First North Americans	North America	Salts	Creative Kids
16	Ancient South America	South America	Plants	South American Art
17	Celts	Europe	Flowering Plants	Jewelry
18	Roman Republic	Asia	Trees	Roman Art
19	Christianity	Australia & Oceania	Simple Plants	Instruments
20	Roman Empire	You Explore	Fungi	Composing Music

2	History	Geography	Science	The Arts
1	Byzantines	Turkey	Climate & Seasons	Byzantine Art
2	Barbarians	Ireland	Forecasting	Illumination
3	Islam	Arabian Peninsula	Clouds & Precipitation	Creative Kids
4	Vikings	Norway	Special Effects	Viking Art
5	Anglo Saxons	Britain	Wild Weather	King Arthur Tales
6	Charlemagne	France	Cells & DNA	Carolingian Art
7	Normans	Nigeria	Skeletons	Canterbury Tales
8	Feudal System	Germany	Muscles, Skin, Cardio	Gothic Art
9	Crusades	Balkans	Digestive & Senses	Religious Art
10	Burgundy, Venice, Spain	Switzerland	Nerves	Oil Paints
11	Wars of the Roses	Russia	Health	Minstrels & Plays
12	Eastern Europe	Hungary	Metals	Printmaking
13	African Kingdoms	Mali	Carbon Chemistry	Textiles
14	Asian Kingdoms	Southeast Asia	Non-metals	Vivid Language
15	Mongols	Caucasus	Gases	Fun With Poetry
16	Medieval China & Japan	China	Electricity	Asian Arts
17	Pacific Peoples	Micronesia	Circuits	Arts of the Islands
18	American Peoples	Canada	Technology	Indian Legends
19	The Renaissance	Italy	Magnetism	Renaissance Art I
20	Explorers	Caribbean Sea	Motors	Renaissance Art II

www.Layers-of-Learning.com

3	History	Geography	Science	The Arts
1	Age of Exploration	Argentina & Chile	Classification & Insects	Fairy Tales
2	The Ottoman Empire	Egypt & Libya	Reptiles & Amphibians	Poetry
3	Mogul Empire	Pakistan & Afghanistan	Fish	Mogul Arts
4	Reformation	Angola & Zambia	Birds	Reformation Art
5	Renaissance England	Tanzania & Kenya	Mammals & Primates	Shakespeare
6	Thirty Years' War	Spain	Sound	Baroque Music
7	The Dutch	Netherlands	Light & Optics	Baroque Art I
8	France	Indonesia	Bending Light	Baroque Art II
9	The Enlightenment	Korean Peninsula	Color	Art Journaling
10	Russia & Prussia	Central Asia	History of Science	Watercolors
11	Conquistadors	Baltic States	Igneous Rocks	Creative Kids
12	Settlers	Peru & Bolivia	Sedimentary Rocks	Native American Art
13	13 Colonies	Central America	Metamorphic Rocks	Settler Sayings
14	Slave Trade	Brazil	Gems & Minerals	Colonial Art
15	The South Pacific	Australasia	Fossils	Principles of Art
16	The British in India	India	Chemical Reactions	Classical Music
17	The Boston Tea Party	Japan	Reversible Reactions	Folk Music
18	Founding Fathers	Iran	Compounds & Solutions	Rococo
19	Declaring Independence	Samoa & Tonga	Oxidation & Reduction	Creative Crafts I
20	The American Revolution	South Africa	Acids & Bases	Creative Crafts II

4	History	Geography	Science	The Arts
1	American Government	USA	Heat & Temperature	Patriotic Music
2	Expanding Nation	Pacific States	Motors & Engines	Tall Tales
3	Industrial Revolution	U.S. Landscapes	Energy	Romantic Art I
4	Revolutions	Mountain West States	Energy Sources	Romantic Art II
5	Africa	U.S. Political Maps	Energy Conversion	Impressionism I
6	The West	Southwest States	Earth Structure	Impressionism II
7	Civil War	National Parks	Plate Tectonics	Post Impressionism
8	World War I	Plains States	Earthquakes	Expressionism
9	Totalitarianism	U.S. Economics	Volcanoes	Abstract Art
10	Great Depression	Heartland States	Mountain Building	Kinds of Art
11	World War II	Symbols & Landmarks	Chemistry of Air & Water	War Art
12	Modern East Asia	The South	Food Chemistry	Modern Art
13	India's Independence	People of America	Industry	Pop Art
14	Israel	Appalachian States	Chemistry of Farming	Modern Music
15	Cold War	U.S. Territories	Chemistry of Medicine	Free Verse
16	Vietnam War	Atlantic States	Food Chains	Photography
17	Latin America	New England States	Animal Groups	Latin American Art
18	Civil Rights	Home State Study I	Instincts	Theater & Film
19	Technology	Home State Study II	Habitats	Architecture
20	Terrorism	America in Review	Conservation	Creative Kids

Unit 4-1

Printable Pack

This unit includes printables at the end. To make life easier for you we also created digital printable packs for each unit. To retrieve your printable pack for Unit 4-1, please visit

www.layers-of-learning.com/digital-printable-packs/

Put the printable pack in your shopping cart and use this coupon code:

0911UNIT4-1

Your printable pack will be free.

Layers of Learning Introduction

This is part of a series of units in the Layers of Learning homeschool curriculum, including the subjects of history, geography, science, and the arts. Children from 1st through 12th can participate in the same curriculum at the same time - family school style.

The units are intended to be used in order as the basis of a complete curriculum (once you add in a systematic math, reading, and writing program). You begin with Year 1 Unit 1 no matter what ages your children are. Spend about 2 weeks on each unit. You pick and choose the activities within the unit that appeal to you and read the books from the book list that are available to you or find others on the same topic from your library. We highly recommend that you use the timeline in every history section as the backbone. Then flesh out your learning with reading and activities that highlight the topics you think are the most important.

Alternatively, you can use the units as activity ideas to supplement another curriculum in any order you wish. You can still use them with all ages of children at the same time.

When you've finished with Year One, move on to Year Two, Year Three, and Year Four. Then begin again with Year One and work your way through the years again. Now your children will be older, reading more involved books, and writing more in depth. When you have completed the sequence for the second time, you start again on it for the third and final time. If your student began with Layers of Learning in 1st grade and stayed with it all the way through she would go through the four year rotation three times, firmly cementing the information in her mind in ever increasing depth. At each level you should expect increasing amounts of outside reading and writing. High schoolers in particular should be reading extensively, and if possible, participating in discussion groups.

These icons will guide you in spotting activities and books that are appropriate for the age of child you are working with. But if you think an activity is too juvenile or too difficult for your kids, adjust accordingly. The icons are not there as rules, just guides.

☺ 1st-4th

☻ 5th-8th

☻ 9th-12th

Within each unit we share:

EXPLORATIONS, activities relating to the topic;
EXPERIMENTS, usually associated with science topics;
EXPEDITIONS, field trips;
EXPLANATIONS, teacher helps or educational philosophies.

In the sidebars we also include Additional Layers, Famous Folks, Fabulous Facts, On the Web, and other extra related topics that can take you off on tangents, exploring the world and your interests with a bit more freedom. The curriculum will always be there to pull you back on track when you're ready.

www.layers-of-learning.com

UNIT ONE

AMERICAN GOVERNMENT – U.S.A. – HEAT & TEMP – PATRIOTIC MUSIC

A wise and frugal Government, which shall restrain men from injuring one another, which shall leave them otherwise free to regulate their own pursuits of industry and improvement, and shall not take from the mouth of labor the bread it has earned. This is the sum of good government . . .
-Thomas Jefferson

LIBRARY LIST

HISTORY	Search for: Constitution, James Madison, Constitutional Convention, American Government, Bill of Rights ☻ We The People by Lynne Cheney. ☻ Hail To The Chief by Don Robb. All about the job of being a president. ☻ ☻ The Bill of Rights (Government in Action) by John Hamilton. ☻ ☻ The Bill of Rights by Syl Sobel J.D. ☻ ☻ Shh! We're Writing the Constitution! by Jean Fritz. ☻ The Great Little Madison by Jean Fritz. ☻ The Founders: The 39 Stories Behind the U.S. Constitution by Denis Brindell Fradin ☻ How To Build Your Own Country by Valerie Wyatt. Kids get to create their own borders, flag, constitution, anthem, and solve all the world's problems in an interactive book. ☻ ☻ The U.S. Constitution For Everyone by Jerome B. Agel and Mort Gerberg. ☻ ☻ Whatever Happened To Justice? by Richard Maybury. ☻ ☻ Whatever Happened To Penny Candy? by Richard Maybury. ☻ ☻ U.S. Constitution in 15 Minutes a Day from Learning Express. Textbook feel, but a decent read. ☻ In Our Defense: The Bill of Rights in Action by Ellen Alderman. ☻ Selected Federalist Papers from Dover Publishers. ☻ The Original Argument by Glenn Beck. Federalist Papers, simplified for today. ☻ The Law by Frederick Bastiat. Written in an easy, accessible style. ☻ The Constitution of the United States. People are intimidated by this, but you shouldn't be; it's not written in lawyerese. It is our document, the People's document. We've included it at the end of this unit as a printable, but you may like it in book form. ☻ Free To Choose by Milton and Rose Friedman. A book about the free market system, how and why it works. Easy to understand. ☻ The Politically Incorrect Guide to the Founding Fathers by Brion T. McClanahan. ☻ The Politically Incorrect Guide to the Constitution by Kevin R. C. Gutzman. ☻ Miracle at Philadelphia by Catherine Drinker Bowen.

GEOGRAPHY	Search for: U.S. States, 50 States, States, United States of America, U.S. Landforms, Time Zones ☺ ☺ ☻ <u>Our Fifty States</u> by Stephen F. Cunha. From National Geographic, great photos, maps, and information for all ages. If you want to buy one book on all fifty states, this is it. ☺ ☺ ☻ <u>National Geographic Atlas For Young Explorers</u>. Worth buying. ☺ ☺ ☻ <u>50 States: A State by State Tour of the U.S.A.</u> by Erin McHugh and Albert Schrier. ☺ ☺ ☻ <u>When It's Six O'Clock in San Francisco: A Trip Through Time Zones</u> by Cynthia Jaynes Omolulu. Shows the concept of time zones through a look at the everyday lives of kids around the globe. ☺ ☺ ☻ <u>U.S. Landforms</u> by Dana Meachen Rau. This book focuses on the natural landforms and landmarks found within the United States. It is very simple and suitable for young kids. ☺ ☺ ☻ <u>Memorize U.S. Geography: On My Way Across The United States</u> by Dr. Julie Schultz. This book serves as a memory aid for kids who want to learn the states. It's the story of a turkey named Burk who is traveling across America. It has little hints for memorization throughout the story.
SCIENCE	Search for: heat, temperature, hot and cold ☺ <u>Why Does Water Evaporate? All About Heat and Temperature</u> by Rob Moore. ☺ <u>The Energy That Warms Us: A Look at Heat</u> by Jennifer Boothroyd. ☺ ☻ <u>How Do We Know The Laws of Thermodynamics? Great Scientific Questions and the Scientists Who Answered Them</u> by Jeffrey Moran. ☻ <u>Basic Physics: A Self Teaching Guide</u> by Karl F. Khun. Read chapters 8 and 9.
THE ARTS	Search for: Star Spangled Banner, America the Beautiful, Battle Hymn of the Republic ☺ ☺ ☻ <u>God Bless America: The Ultimate Patriotic Album</u>. Music CD ☺ ☺ ☻ <u>America the Beautiful</u> illust. Wendell Minor. Uses the text of the Bates song. ☺ ☺ ☻ <u>The Power of Patriotism: Featuring the Story of Francis Scott Key</u> by DeLynn Decker. This is intended for kids and told in story form. It would make a great read aloud for kids of all ages. ☺ <u>Wee Sing America</u>. Geared especially for younger kids, includes a song that will have you memorizing the fifty states with ease. ☺ <u>The Story of the Star Spangled Banner</u> by Patricia A. Pingry and Nancy Munger. ☺ ☻ <u>Francis Scott Key's Star Spangled Banner</u> by Monica Kulling and Richard Walz. ☺ ☻ <u>The Star Spangled Banner</u> illust. By Peter Spier.

HISTORY: AMERICAN GOVERNMENT

After the American colonies declared their independence from Britain, they knew they had to work together and fight as a unified political group and under a unified army or they could never hope for enough power to succeed, so the first thing they did was create a national government. The first document that governed the charter of the national government was called the Articles of Confederation.

This is a painting of Washington leading the Constitutional Convention by Junius Brutus Stearns, 1856.

After the war most people were content to let the Articles of Confederation continue in their role while the states went back to the actual art of governing, but not James Madison. He wrote letters and letters and letters to all his friends he had met while serving in the congress and finally managed to convince several of them that they should take another look at the national government. Madison thought the Articles were too weak, that many of the problems that existed during the Revolutionary War, like the soldiers not getting paid or having supplies, could have been avoided if the congress had power to tax, for example. Also after the Revolution states began to have problems with one another like who had to pay for which section of road and whether Rhode Island could tax goods coming in from other states.

Madison called the first convention in 1786, but only five states delegates showed up so all they accomplished was a letter requesting a Constitutional Convention for the following year be sent to all the state legislatures. Finally they got some interest and in the summer of 1787 delegates, duly appointed by the state legislatures, from 12 states (Rhode Island boycotted the whole harebrained scheme) met in Philadelphia to discuss the forming of a new nation. The delegates were given permission by their states to amend or revise the Articles of Confederation, but James Madison had something entirely different in mind.

Before the convention began Madison spent the winter months writing a first draft of what he thought would be a good plan for a national government. After a short time the other delegates agreed; they would write a brand new document and completely scrap the Articles of Confederation. Madison's plan was what they started with, arguing over every little bit until they could at least mostly agree. Several other people and groups wrote up their own ideas, challenging Madison, they argued, compromised, gave a little and took a little and finally they wrote up a final draft, which was sent to the states for approval.

Then Madison really got to work along with his friends John Jay and Alexander Hamilton. Their next job was to sell the Constitution to the people of the United States, because it was nothing but ideas on paper until the state legislatures ratified the document and made it the law of the land. Jay, Hamilton, and Madison wrote the Federalist Papers, articles that were published in newspapers all over the country that presented the argument for why each item was placed in the Constitution and what it all meant. We don't have to guess what their original intentions were, they told us.

☺ ☺ ☺ EXPLORATION: Timeline
At the end of this unit you will find printable timeline squares.
- Summer 1776 Articles of Confederation drafted
- 1781 Articles of Confederation finally ratified
- September 1786 Annapolis Convention of five States meets
- Summer 1787 Constitutional Convention in Philadelphia
- September 17, 1787 Constitution is signed by the delegates
- June 21, 1788 The Constitution takes effect with the ratification of New Hampshire, the ninth state
- April 30, 1789 George Washington is sworn in as the First President
- 1791 The Bill of Rights is added to the Constitution

☺ ☺ EXPLORATION: Types of Government
The most basic political argument we have today is how much government should we have? Should the government make sure we don't starve? Should the government make sure we have our

Additional Layer

The bald eagle is a symbol of America, after the ancient Roman symbol of an eagle.

The eagle appears on seals, stamps, currency, and other places. Learn more about this bird.

Famous Folks

Charles Pinckney of South Carolina had also written a document of his vision of an American national government, but Madison was a better organizer and already had a group of supporters together so Pinckney got steamrolled.

On the Web

http://www.archives. gov/exhibits/charters/ constitution.html

Go see what the original document of the Constitution looks like, read the transcribed text and read the excellent questions and answers page when you go to the link above.

Fabulous Fact

The Founders were all highly educated and extremely well-read men. They knew all about the ancient Roman Republic, the Greek attempts at government, the history of British rights and freedoms, and the more recent attempts at freedom that were happening in the Netherlands and Germany.

They had read Plato and Aristotle, Cicero and Plutarch, Montesquieu and John Locke. They had read the magna carta, the English Bill of Rights, their own colonial charters, and more than half of them had studied law as a profession. They were up on more current events too like the new book out by Adam Smith on capitalism and economic freedom and the phenomenal compilation and argument for English common law put out by Blackstone.

They knew history, philosophy, law, and above all human nature. They were men of faith, every one of them having studied the Bible from infancy. And it was all this knowledge upon which they based their ideas about American government.

medical bills paid for? Should the government tell us which foods we can and can't eat or tell us whether we should smoke or drink alcohol or do drugs? Should the government tell us who we can and can't marry? And how much of our money should the government be allowed to take? We even have people today who argue that we should have no government. If these sound like current events, they are, but they're also eternal events, things that the Founders argued over as well.

Here is the Founders view of government, how they would have visualized it and where they thought the proper level of government lay.

On the extreme left we have a totalitarian government, a government that has absolute power. In their day they called it an absolute monarchy, in our day we call it a dictatorship, but it's the same thing really. On the far right of the scale we have no government at all, an anarchy.

To the right of center we placed the form of government called a republic, this is the degree of government the Founders decided was the proper one. Enough government to protect the property and lives of the citizens both from internal criminals and from foreign threats and enough to facilitate trade both foreign and domestic, but not so much that the people were oppressed. They were aiming for the balance of true freedom. You can not be free with no government, because you must spend all your time and resources protecting your person and property from bullies. Neither can you be free if the government becomes the bully, claiming a legal right to take your life or property.

Look up the definitions of the three main types of government: Totalitarianism, Anarchy, and Republic. Make a list of the pros and cons of each type of government.

Learn more about the different forms of government and economic systems by playing the government match game. You'll find a printable below and also at http://www.layers-of-learning.com/government-types-for-kids/.

☻ EXPLORATION: Articles of Confederation
The Articles of Confederation were very careful and cautious

against giving the national government too much power. The states, in creating a governing body were very afraid it would take over and destroy the power and sovereignty of the states, so it was weak on purpose. It could not tax the states, and in order for any legislation to take effect the states all had to be unanimous in their decisions. Whatever the Confederation decided, they could not enforce any of their decisions on the states. Sound too good to be true? Maybe it was.

It made for very tough conditions to fight a war under. Imagine the problems if some of the states today agreed we should go to war or even if all of them did, but then only a fourth of them actually agreed to give any money over to the government with which to fight it.

The thinking of course is that if the war were actually in the interest of the state then it would pay up, but that fond belief does not take into account the human desire to get something for nothing. During the Revolution many states were not terribly concerned with footing their portion of the bill.

Then too, no treaties with foreign nations could be entirely relied on since the states could not be forced to comply. What problems do you think this could cause?

Visit the site link below and first look at the image of the actual Articles of Confederation document and then click on the link to read the transcribed Articles of Confederation. As you read them together, create a list of powers that the confederation had and powers that the states retained. Save your list to compare to the Constitution.

http://www.ourdocuments.gov/doc.php?flash=true&doc=3#

What does Article I mean? Was that idea retained in the Constitution or not?

☺ EXPLORATION: Madison
Color the picture of James Madison that you will find at the end of this unit. Print the page of quotes and cut them out, pasting them around Madison's head. Talk about each idea as you go and discuss what Madison meant, whether you agree or disagree, and why.

☺ ☺ Natural Laws and Natural Rights
The Constitution is based on the idea that all people have natural rights that must be protected and that the reason we have government is to protect these rights.

Deep Thoughts
John Locke may be the most important of the philosophers to influence the founders. High schoolers should read his *Two Treatises on Government.* SparkNotes can help: http://www.sparknotes.com/philosophy/johnlocke/section2.rhtml

Additional Layer
Look up Shays Rebellion and find out what it had to do with the Articles of Confederation.

http://shaysrebellion.stcc.edu/index.html

Think about this:

The rebels had just thrown off the government of the British through armed conflict and yet to a man the Revolutionary War leaders condemned the men who tried to do the same to their Massachusetts government when it governed badly. Were they power hungry hypocrites or was there a real difference?

Deep Thoughts

Where does the government get its power? In America we say it is from the people. If the power is from the people then government can have no powers that individual people do not have.

You can always run this test to see if a law or practice of the government is just.

Could I as an individual morally do what the government is doing?

If not, then the government has strayed from the rights given by the people and become a tyranny, at least in that one instance. People cannot grant to government powers that they do not themselves possess.

So what rights and powers do individuals have? The right to protect life and property are the most fundamental.

Thomas Jefferson said, "The legitimate powers of government extend to such acts only as are injurious to others. But it does me no injury for my neighbor to say there are twenty gods, or no god. It neither picks my pocket nor breaks my leg."

Philosophers often imagine a "natural state" or a condition of mankind before there was society and governments. This helps us to understand what "Natural Rights" people have and how they can interact without destroying the rights of others.

Imagine your family just packed up and headed into the wilderness in a place far from civilization. Pretty soon other families also settle in your area. Then the neighbor down the river finds some of his cattle have been stolen. What can be done about this?

You are currently living in a state of anarchy, or no government. You can continue in the state of anarchy and the offended farmer can spend his time and resources searching for his cattle and punishing the thief or the community can vote in a sheriff to bring about justice.

- What are the consequences if the farmer punishes the thief himself?
- What are the consequences of hiring a sheriff?
- And who says it's wrong to steal cattle in the first place?

In the case stated above, the settlers, even the thief, would probably agree that stealing is wrong. In this example everyone has a common morality. Where does this morality come from? There are two possibilities.

1. From an individual or group who decide what is right and wrong for the whole of society.
2. From God, or the universe, or what have you, an ultimate, infallible, constant authority.

Alexander Hamilton agreed with virtually all of the Founders when he said, "The sacred rights of mankind are not to be rummaged for, among old parchments or musty records. They are written, as with a sun beam, in the volume of human nature, by the hand of divinity itself; and can never be erased or obscured by mortal power."

If morality, and hence law, comes from human beings then the law is subject to the whims of imperfect human beings. But law based on the morals of a supreme being is immutable and unchangeable.

The reason people have equal value and rights as human beings is because those rights are given to all human beings by God.

Again we turn to Alexander Hamilton, "The fundamental source of all your errors, sophisms and false reasonings is a total ignorance of the natural rights of mankind. Were you once to become acquainted with these, you could never entertain a thought, that all men are not, by nature, entitled to a parity of privileges. You would be convinced, that natural liberty is a gift of the beneficent Creator to the whole human race, and that civil liberty is founded in that; and cannot be wrested from any people, without the most manifest violation of justice."

People often say that morality cannot be legislated and yet all laws are based on some morality or another.

- Think of some examples of laws. Whose morality are these laws based on? Is the law a good law or a bad one? Does it pass the test of the sidebar on the left?

As soon as the settlers in our example hire a sheriff they have formed a government.

- Write up a code of laws for your imaginary settlement. Include eight to twelve of the most important ones.
- Why did you include the laws you did?
- Where does the power for each of the laws come from? Does each of the laws represent something that an individual would have the power to do?

Power over people can be gotten in ways other than consent. Force through armies, weapons, threats, secret police and fear have also been used to gain power over people. These are the only two choices. Government either rules with the consent of the governed or it rules through brutal force.

☺ ☺ ☺ EXPLORATION: Preamble
Every part of the Constitution was written with specific words and meanings, including the Preamble. Here we'll go through it phrase by phrase and explain it.

We the People of the United States,. . .
The Constitution comes from the people, the power comes from the people, the government exists at the sufferance and will of the people. This is an important difference between a republic and almost every other form of government. Usually a group or individual takes power by force and exerts it over others, but as our Declaration said "all men are created equal, they are endowed by their Creator with unalienable Rights . . . that to secure these Rights governments are instituted among men." The founders understood that people often took power by force and trampled on the rights of their fellow man, but they also understood that this is an offense to natural law and that those who offended the rights of man would be held accountable. If there is no God, then of course there are also no rights, unless they are granted by a benevolent government, which can then take them away.

. . . in order to form a more perfect Union,

Additional Layer

Governments are given power so they can fulfill their responsibilities to protect individuals.

What do you think some of the specific duties of government consist of?

Explanation

Some who read this section might be tempted to think we are trying to force religion on them. We are not.

We are pointing out the logical alternatives to some of the most basic of philosophies regarding power, rights, and government. We are also pointing out what the founders actually thought and said about these topics. If you disagree with the idea that rights come from God, then you ought to teach your kids where you disagree and why.

We do however think you ought to seriously consider the options. As Thomas Jefferson said, "A free people claim their rights from the laws of nature, and not as the gift of their chief magistrate."

Since we believe with our whole hearts in human freedom we stand with natural rights as the basis of all human liberty.

Additional Layer

John Adams said, "If there is a form of government, then, whose principle and foundation is virtue, will not every sober man acknowledge it better calculated to promote the general happiness than any other form?"

A republic is dependent on the virtue, or morality, of the citizens. Adams believes this is more likely to lead to happiness than a government that forces good behavior.

The truth is that freedom can only exist where people can control themselves. If an individual cannot control himself then he must be controlled by someone else.

A humorous example of this principle is that in Fairbanks, Alaska a law is on the books stating that it is illegal to get a moose drunk. The only problem is that of course someone did get a moose drunk and so a law had to be made about it. As people do stupid or harmful things we get more and more laws and lose more and more freedom.

Additional Layer

Watch "The Birth of the Constitution", a Charlie Brown video, for kids.

Now we see here listed the reasons the Constitution was created. The first reason is to make sure the states, which were in every sense separate sovereign countries, would remain united. The main reason they needed to be united and not remain separate was for defense from foreign (European) nations, but also because they could grow more wealthy trading freely with one another than they could if they were in competition with one another.

. . . establish Justice, . . .
The new government would have a law making role and through the judicial system would be the last resort for the upholding of the rights of the people in case any state or body within the states became corrupt.

. . . insure domestic Tranquility, . . .
The federal government has a role to play in putting down uprisings, and solving disputes between states or between citizens of different states, whether that dispute is legal, economic, or armed.

. . . provide for the common defense, . . .
Common means as a whole. If any foreign nation or entity were to make war against the United States or any part of the United States then the Federal Government's job is to defend the nation.

. . . promote the general Welfare, . . .
This may be the most misunderstood phrase in the Constitution. It does not mean "take care of individuals". The term "welfare" didn't mean charity or a handout until politicians hijacked the word from the Constitution and changed its meaning to excuse the new unconstitutional charity programs they were creating in the 1930's. "General Welfare", simply means to take measures that will benefit the States as a whole (hence the word "general"); it certainly has absolutely nothing to do with individual citizens.

. . . and secure the Blessings of Liberty to ourselves and our Posterity, . . .
The point of the Constitution was get it all down in writing so that not only the present generation, but all those who came after could understand the role of the federal government, and most especially understand that unless government was constrained and limited the people would not have liberty.

. . . do ordain and establish this Constitution for the United States of America.
Ordain means to give sacred authority to wield power. Establish means to set in place firmly or unalterably. So the founders intended the Constitution to last as the supreme law of the land above and outside the power of man to abolish.

Now go memorize the preamble with this awesome classic Schoolhouse Rock video: http://youtu.be/3OOyU4O8oi4

☻☻ EXPLORATION: Three Branches

The Constitution established three branches of the federal government and tells us exactly which powers the federal government has. At the end of this unit you will find printables that show the three branches and what their role is in government. Cut them out and arrange them on a table or paste them onto cardstock and put them in a binder.

☻☻ EXPLORATION: Constitutional Authority

Using a copy of the Constitution (you will find one at the end of this unit) go through the "Three Branches by the Constitution" worksheet.

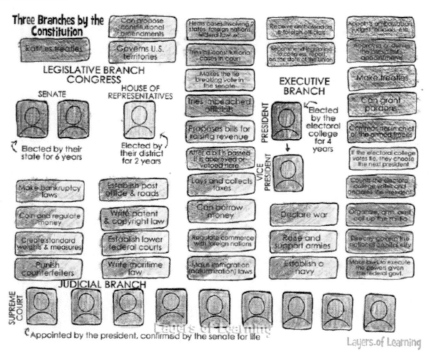

Additional Layer

The history behind the Constitution and Bill of Rights is crucial to understanding them, so read up on the Founders.

On the Web

This blogger created some printables to help kids with the Preamble: http://thewisenest.com/preamble-constitution.html

Explanation

In history text books again and again you see the phrase "The Articles of Confederation were too weak". That my friends is a value judgment, not necessarily a fact. Read more about it and decide for yourself.

Personally we agree with that statement. In a day of out of control government it can be tempting to pine for the days when the feds were weak, but we forget that we would still have tyrants, they would just sit in the state capital instead of the national.

What the Constitution did was set up a system of checks and balances, not only within the federal government, but between the federal government and states and it is oh, so elegantly done.

Famous Folks

James Madison, known as the Father of the Constitution, was also the fourth president of the United States. His home was on a Virginia plantation known as Montpelier. You can visit his home online or in person: https://www.montpelier.org/

Weighing in at less than 100 pounds James Madison was also our only president to personally lead troops into battle while president of the United States.

Additional Layer

Learn how an amendment to the Constitution may be adopted. At any given time there are several amendments under discussion. Find out about one and consider whether such an amendment would benefit and protect the freedom of the people or not.

Each of the powers granted to the federal government are written in the boxes on the worksheet. Color code each box to show which entity of the government has the specific power mentioned. The legislative branch should have two colors in the same color family to designate it, like orange and yellow, and the president and vice president should also have two colors in the same color family to represent them, like dark blue and light blue. The Supreme Court justices can all be in the same color, like green. Many of the legislative functions are shared by the House and Senate, these can be colored with both orange and yellow.

If you like you can obtain and print portraits of each of the people currently in office to paste into the boxes. Images should be about 80x100 pixels and can be re-sized with photo editing software or using Microsoft Paint.

☻ ☻ EXPLORATION: Checks and Balances

As the Constitutional Convention met in the hot sticky summer of 1887 in Philadelphia they behaved like politicians. Some got bored and went home, others left in a huff, refusing to have anything further to do with the whole thing and the rest who stayed argued and squabbled through the whole process. Finally they gave a little, took a little, compromised a little, did some convincing and did some learning, and came up with the document we now know as the Constitution.

Benjamin Franklin, ever wise and reflective, summed up how they all felt about the final product, "I confess that there are several parts of this constitution which I do not at present approve, but I am not sure I shall never approve them: For having lived long, I have experienced many instances of being obliged by better information, or fuller consideration, to change opinions even on important subjects, which I once thought right, but found to be otherwise . . . It therefore astonishes me, Sir, to find this system approaching so near to perfection as it does; and I think it will astonish our enemies . . . Thus I consent, Sir, to this Constitution because I expect no better, and because I am not sure, that it is not the best.

Read Ben's full speech to the President of the Congress here: http://www.usconstitution.net/franklin.html

Indeed the final product of the Constitution is astonishing in its system of checks and balances, in its intricacy in preserving the liberty of the people and constraining the power of government, all with an elegant simplicity. Especially astonishing is the result when you consider that this was the first attempt of mankind since the old Roman Republic in such a project, that of creating a perpetual government that would be ruled not by powerful men, but by the people themselves.

In most textbooks you see a simple diagram that looks something like this:

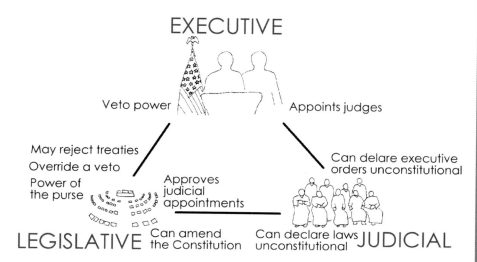

EXECUTIVE

Veto power | Appoints judges

May reject treaties
Override a veto
Power of the purse
Approves judicial appointments

Can delare executive orders unconstitutional

LEGISLATIVE   Can amend the Constitution   Can declare laws unconstitutional   JUDICIAL

This shows how the different branches of the federal government have the tools to jealously guard their power from the others, but while this is true, it is only the beginning. The real point of the checks and balances is not to help one set of politicians retain power over another, it is to preserve the power of the people. Instead of speaking of the three branches of the federal government we need to speak of the checks between the Federal, State, and People.

At the end of this unit you will find a chart that shows the checks and balances in our system of government. They are listed as powers that each of the entities possesses. Following the chart there is an explanation of some of the powers and also a discussion on how those checks and balances and the power of the people can be and are threatened. Read the information together and discuss it. Refer to the Constitution as you read and discuss.

☺ ☺ ☺ EXPLORATION: Bill of Rights
Even though we call the first ten amendments a "Bill of Rights", it's really a bill of restrictions. The Constitution never pretends to grant anything to the people. Remember the people already have all the rights and all the power. The Constitution tells the federal government exactly what it can and can not do. So the Bill of Rights tells the government that it can not make any laws in these specific areas.

Additional Layer

A federal system means that a group of sovereign nations come together and form a national government which has specific and limited authority which will govern and benefit the several states, while the states retain most of their powers.

In the United States, fifty individual states are federated under a national government, which is above the states only in the specific powers granted by the Constitution, all other powers, as stated in the tenth amendment, belong to the states.

Explanation

Those who were against a bill of rights feared that by listing a few rights the government would then proceed to violate any and all rights not listed.

Those who were for a bill of rights thought government was not to be trusted unless specifically restrained in at least the most important ways.

The compromise was the ninth amendment which clearly states that just because it's not listed doesn't mean it's not a right of the people. The people hold <u>all</u> rights and <u>all</u> power.

Additional Layer

Nearly every country on earth now has a written Constitution and a document protecting the rights of their citizens. They are all modeled to some extent on the American Constitution and Bill of Rights. It can be helpful to see how the American form of government has blessed the world.

Go read about some of the governments and constitutions of foreign nations. Are they living up to the ideals of the American Constitution? Are we in America living up to those ideals?

On the Web

You can explore the First Amendment further at Layers of Learning: http://www.layers-of-learning.com/the-first-amendment-for-kids/

We also have information on the Second Amendment: http://www.layers-of-learning.com/the-second-amendment-for-kids/

And the Tenth Amendment: http://www.layers-of-learning.com/the-tenth-amendment-for-kids/

There were two sides debating whether to include a Bill of Rights in the Constitution. The final draft did not include one, and many states refused to sign, but they finally did when they received a promise that the first act of the new government would be to pass a Bill of Rights. It was one of the few promises ever kept by politicians.

Before you read the Bill of Rights with your kids take some time to read them yourself and think them over. They truly are written in plain English, it does not take a legal mind to understand them or a judge to interpret them.

Play a matching game to help your kids become familiar with and memorize the Bill of Rights. Use the cards from the end of this unit, printed onto card stock, and cut out. Place the cards upside down on a table and try to get matches by turning over two at a time.

☻ ☻ ☻ **EXPLORATION: More Amendments**
Make an open-the-flap page about some of the other amendments to the Constitution. Look them up, discuss what they mean and then draw a picture of what you think it means on a 3"x5" piece of card stock. Glue down one edge of the card onto another full sheet of card stock. Under the flap you have created write the number and text of the amendment. Several amendments will fit on one page. You can quiz yourself to see if you can remember what each amendment is about. Older kids can do more amendments than young kids.

☻ ☻ ☻ **EXPLORATION: Parts of the Constitution**
Make a "film strip" page to show the parts of the Constitution. First cut a sheet of paper in half the long way, hot dog style. Tape the two halves together end to end to make one long strip. Divide the strip into ten equal parts. Leave the first and last section of the strip blank so that as you are pulling the "film strip" through the page it doesn't come out all the way. Title the remaining eight sections: Article 1, Article 2, Article 3, Article 4, Article 5, Article 6, Article 7, and Amendments. Write a short description and/or draw illustrations in each section showing what that part of the Constitution talks about.

Then on a full size sheet of card stock draw two lines in the center of the page, parallel to one another and far enough apart to just fit one frame of your "film strip" at a time. Then cut slits in the paper along these lines and wide enough to fit your film strip through. At the top of the paper title the page "The Constitution". Copy the preamble onto the page above the slits for the "film strip". Finally slide the long paper strip through the slits from the back to the front and then back out to the back so that one frame of the "film strip shows at a time. You can pull the strip through to read about the parts of the Constitution.

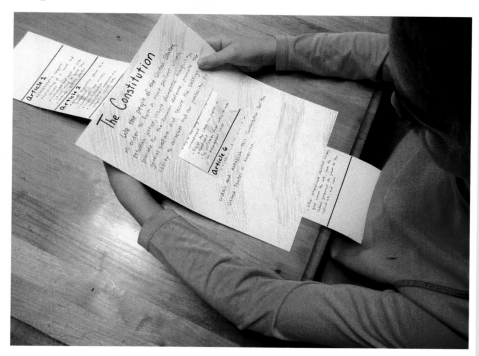

☺ ☻ EXPLORATION: Constitutional Liberty

Make a liberty themed painting with the liberty torch in the center and a background of the American flag. On the torch write "The Constitution protects my liberty and my neighbor's."

You can use this tutorial on drawing the liberty torch:

http://www.dragoart.com/tuts/16960/1/1/how-to-draw-a-torch,-liberty-torch.htm.

But leave the flames as an outline so that you will be able to write the words in that space. Then paint in the flag background. Write the words in after the painting dries.

Additional Layers

The *Federalist Papers* were essays written by Alexander Hamilton, James Madison, and John Jay and published in newspapers throughout the United States.

The purpose of the essays was to explain the Constitution and gather support from the people so the Constitution could be ratified by the state legislatures.

Today these writings are extremely valuable as we try to apply the Constitution to our laws and government.

Older teens should read at least parts of the Federalist Papers. Layers of Learning has a guided tour of several of the most relevant Federalist Papers. They can answer our questions and clarify the application of the Constitution.

http://www.layers-of-learning.com/a-teachers-guide-to-the-federalist-papers/

Additional Layer

Just because you can doesn't mean you should.

Sure you have freedom of speech, but that doesn't mean you should say anything that pops into your brain, no matter how hurtful it might be.

GEOGRAPHY: UNITED STATES OF AMERICA

Additional Layer

Review some geography terms by finding examples of these features in the United States:

coastal plain
mountain range
plains
drainage system
basin
peninsula
cape
valley
plateau

You can add others to this list if you wish.

This is a picture of the Great Basin, an area high in the Rocky Mountains with no drainage to the sea. Image by Larry Crist, CC license, Wikimedia.

More Maps

You can use one of the maps of the United States from the printables section of this unit to create maps that show climate, rainfall, physiography, altitude, terrain, natural landscapes, natural landmarks, river systems, animal or plant distributions, or drainage basins.

The United States of America covers the central portion of the North American continent from the Pacific to the Atlantic. It contains landscapes ranging from boreal forests to tropical beaches and from deserts to coastal swamps.

Along the eastern side of the country is a long wide coastal plain, rich land for farming in the south, and plentiful deep water ports for trade in the north. Just inland a hundred miles or so is a long mountain range running from the north to the south. These are the Appalachians. They are old mountains, low and rounded, covered with woodlands, and teeming with wild life.

Across the mountains is a huge drainage basin covered with native forests, but today much of this area has been cleared for farmland. Major river systems such as the Ohio, the Tennessee, and the Mississippi drain this section of the continent.

The Mississippi is the largest river system in North America and nearly divides the country in two, north to south. West of the Mississippi the land dries out and the center of the continent is covered with vast prairies which have been utilized as farmland, producing enough food to feed the entire world.

The western half of the country is much more rugged than the east with the great Rocky Mountain range forming the continental divide and the spine of the continent. Once across the Rockies, there is an area of desert that ranges from the cool temperate deserts of Washington and Oregon to the hot cacti deserts of the southwest. Along the coast there is another set of mountain ranges that keep the rain from the Pacific hugged along the coast, creating fertile farmland in the south and rain forests in the north.

Politically the United States is divided into fifty states. Within each state there are further divisions of counties (or parishes in Louisiana) and cities. Each state has its own constitution and its own capital. There is also a federal capital called Washington D.C., located on land outside any of the states. Washington D.C. is located in the east on the border between Maryland and Virginia.

In addition to the states there are five inhabited territories of the Unites States including Puerto Rico, Guam, Northern Marianas, United States Virgin Islands, and American Samoa.

☺ ☺ ☺ EXPLORATION: Big Map

At the end of this unit you will find a U.S. map divided onto two pages. Print the pages, trim the left hand side of the second half of the map (the eastern U.S.) and glue it to the left hand side of the map. Then tape along the back of the map to make a firm seal between the two halves. You can then hole punch the map, fold it in half and keep it in a binder. Alternately, you can glue the two halves to a file folder, creating a booklet style map to use throughout the year.

You will work on completing this map all through this year as you study the states. This week label the Pacific and Atlantic Oceans and the Gulf of Mexico. Color these bodies of water in blue. Also look up the location of the United States on a world map or globe. Make sure your younger kids can find it by themselves and that they know it is on the continent of North America.

Point out to your children that Alaska and Hawaii are not actually located south of California, Arizona, and New Mexico. Explain about insets on maps and why Hawaii and Alaska are placed there on printable maps and maps in books. Make sure you look at where they are actually located on a map of the world or a globe.

Take some time to pour over the United States map in your student atlas. Take note of things your kids find interesting so you can go into more depth on those later or discuss them as they come up.

☺ ☺ EXPLORATION: Largest Cities in the United States

At the end of this unit you'll find a printable map of the Unit-

Teaching Tip

In this unit get kids to pour over maps of the United States by having them create scavenger hunts of things on the map for each other. Can you find the Absaroka Range, the Republican River, or Moosehead Lake? Have them swap lists and see who can find and mark each item on a blank map first.

Fabulous Fact

The U.S. is very large and contains nearly every climate type and nearly every terrain type within its borders. You can visit both tropical beaches and polar climes.

Additional Layer

This is an image of the United States at night courtesy of NASA.

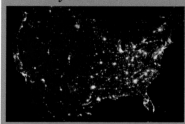

What can you tell about the population of the United States by looking at this image? Given what you know of American history and geography, why do you think the light and dark spaces are located here?

ed States. Use it to look up and mark the locations of cities with 500,000 people or more. Label the cities.

☺ EXPLORATION: Capital Cities

At this end of this unit is a map of the United States. Use a student atlas to write in the names of the capital cities.

Begin to memorize the states and capitals. Once kids have the states and capitals memorized you can use this map again to quiz them, whether that is next week or six months from now.

☺ ☺ EXPLORATION: Postal Codes

The United States Postal Service has designated two letter codes to represent each state when addressing an envelope. You should be familiar with these postal codes. They are used many other places besides when addressing letters, such as on a weather report or on a political map at election time. They're used in advertising or purchasing information when designating which states cannot receive shipments of certain items and so forth.

You can also use the blank map of the United States to fill in the postal codes with the help of an atlas. See how many you can fill in from memory.

We also have printable postal code cards you can use to play a memory game: http://www.layers-of-learning.com/us-postal-codes/.

☺ ☺ EXPLORATION: Time Zones

At the end of this unit you will find a time zone map of the United States. Color each of the time zones in a different color. While the kids color, talk about how time zones work and what they're for. Then ask them questions about the map they made.

We have time zones because the earth is a sphere. As it turns the sun is high in different places on earth at different times. If everyone had the same time then 6:00 AM would be morning for some people, late in the day for others and the middle of the night for others. People want 6:00 AM to mean early morning, so we adjust the time of day according to where people live on the earth.

The United States has six time zones. Hawaii, Alaska, Pacific, Mountain, Central, and Eastern. When it is six o'clock in Hawaii it is seven o'clock in Alaska and eight o'clock in California. In California the sun is higher in the sky than it is in Hawaii so this makes sense.

The time zone lines on the map aren't straight. This is because people who live in nearby cities like to have the same time zone for convenience. North Idaho, for example, is in Pacific time even though the rest of the state, directly south, is in Mountain time

because North Idaho is closely tied to Spokane, Washington, the nearest big city, but almost cut off from Southern Idaho.

Which time zone do you live in?

If it is 5:00 PM in Seattle, what time is it in New York?

Atlanta is how many hours ahead of Anchorage?

If you leave Dallas at 5:00 in the morning and it takes you 11 hours driving time, at what time do you arrive in Atlanta?

If you want to call your grandma in Honolulu at 5:00 pm (her time) and you live in Minneapolis, at what time should you call?

☺ ☺ ☺ EXPLORATION: Photo Collage

Create a photo collage of at least four different regions of the United States. The collage could be arranged on a piece of poster board, on card stock that fits in a notebook, in a digital photo album, as a slide show, or some other medium. Make sure the photos are labeled to show which part of the United States they are from. You could consider these regions: Pacific Northwest, Southwest, Great Plains, Rocky Mountains, Northwest, Great Lakes, Appalachian, and the South. The photos can show natural landscapes and/or cities and people.

Exploration

To illustrate time zones across the world make a series of clocks for different global cities. Clocks can be made from paper plates, construction paper hands, and brads. Make one of the clocks for your home town. Set your clock to your local time. Then ask, "What time is it in London right now? What do you think the people are doing?" And so on.

On the Web

This site has several videos, explanations, and maps about time zones:

http://www.online-mathlearning.com/time-zones.html.

This video is an excellent intro to time zones:

https://youtu.be/-j-SWKtWEcU.

Fabulous Fact

There are no set regions of the United States. Different people group states differently. How would you group the states?

Additional Layer

If you get really into creating your game you can actually have it "published" in the real world for other people to buy. Try this site: https://www.thegamecrafter.com/. You can create a board game or a card game using this site.

Note to parents: Some of the games created by users on this site are definitely not for children. Please explore the site with your kids or do the web stuff yourself.

Additional Layer

Many people think that the time of discovery of new species is over. The truth is that biologists are still in the field looking for new animals and plants, and they are finding them in large numbers.

Read this page to learn more: http://www.allaboutwildlife.com/posts/newly-discovered-animal-species/4162.

On the Web

This is a short video about animals that are unique to the United States: https://youtu.be/TFRMRgTqyMs.

The purpose of this project is to help kids become familiar with the overall landscape and culture of the different parts of the United States. You might pair this with some reading or video clips about the regions or natural features or tourist attractions in these places.

☺ ☺ ☺ EXPLORATION: Create A Game

Create a game based around a map of the United States. We recommend drawing a map of the United States freehand on a piece of poster board then adding a path to travel along, stops to make, spaces for cards to sit and so on. Alternatively you can create a card game or trivia game. The game should include elements that help the players learn about the United States geography. So have landmarks, rivers, mountains, man-made points of interest or major cities included as well.

☺ ☺ ☺ EXPLORATION: Animal Note Card Flip Book

Research to find out what kinds of wild animals live in the United States. Create a flip book of these animals using 3" x 5" note cards and a book ring.

Each note card should include a picture of the animal, either pasted on or drawn on, and a description of the animal and where it lives. Young kids should include at least 8 animals, middle grades kids should include 12 or more, and older kids should include 20 or more animals. In addition, older kids should have more detailed information on the animals than younger kids.

☺ ☺ ☺ EXPLORATION: USA Illustrated Fact Sheet

Using a piece of card stock, create an illustrated fact sheet of the United States of America. Research some facts about the country, draw pictures, maps, or charts to go with the facts you learn and then caption the images. You can make this a single sheet and spend less than an hour or you can expand the project, making several pages each on a different topics such as: landmarks, demographics, symbols, government, and physical geography.

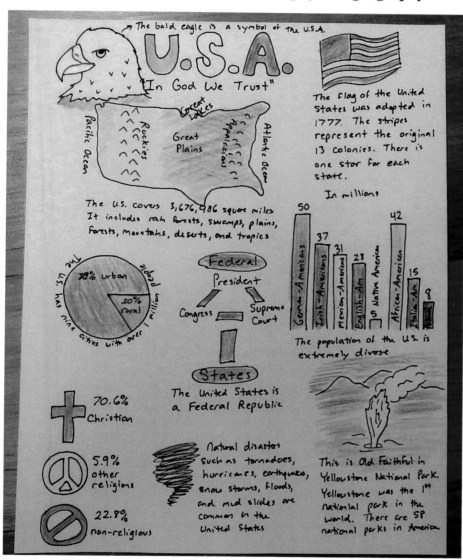

☺ ☺ ☺ EXPLORATION: American Culture

American culture includes foods like hot dogs and pizza, entertainment like Hollywood movies and football, and clothes like blue jeans and T-shirts. There are many other aspects of American culture including literature, national heroes, national holidays, political attitudes, and the Christian religion. But America is also a very

Writer's Workshop

Research the term "American Exceptionalism." In a paper, describe what American Exceptionalism is, then argue in support of or against the theory. Be sure to use concrete examples from American history, politics, and current events to back up your argument.

A great extension on this writing assignment is to write two convincing papers, one for and one against. Practicing taking both sides of an argument makes you a better thinker.

Fabulous Facts

You probably know the basic facts about population and symbols, etc. But see if you can find some obscure facts about the United States of America.

Did you know?

The seven points on the crown of the statue of liberty represent the seven continents.

Congress forgot to hold a vote to admit Ohio to the Union in 1803. The vote wasn't held until 1953.

The Declaration of Independence was written on hemp paper.

Additional Layer

Cultural literacy means having a familiarity with the values, stories, literature, figures, songs, and art that make up your culture. When you are reading or watching a performance a culturally literate person understands the quotations and references made by the author or creator of the piece.

You help children become culturally literate by reading them traditional stories, fairy tales, and fables, listening to music, learning about heroes, reading great literature as they grow, and learning about art together. Most of cultural literacy happens naturally through family life and education. The best way to help your kids? Read aloud.

Deep Thoughts

Sometimes, because American culture is both inherited and so pervasive across the world, Americans are left feeling as though they don't have a culture. Are blue jeans really cultural if everyone wears them? Are hot dogs and pizza really American culture when they were adapted from other places?

diverse place with people from cultures and traditions from all over the world. So while Christmas is an American holiday, not every American celebrates, and some celebrate holidays like Hanukkah which are not considered mainstream.

These things are all part of American culture: rock 'n roll, Paul Bunyan, burgers and fries, Christian churches, baseball, liberty, Hollywood, Broadway plays, blue jeans, Santa Claus, Davy Crockett, and state fairs. Photo of Bruce Springsteen by Craig ONeal, CC license, the remaining images are public domain.

Certain aspects of American culture have been spread across the world to many different cultures. For example, blue jeans and t-shirts are the casual wear for people across the globe, Hollywood movies are subtitled and watched everywhere, and American music is played on radio stations in places as far flung as Finland and Argentina.

Make a presentation about American culture. It could be a research paper, a poster board display, a video or slide show, a display of items, a collage, or a speech. You should have examples of American culture in several or all of these categories: religion, fables and stories, national heroes, important events, symbols, clothing, music, fine art, food, holidays, national character, political attitudes, literature, traditions, landmarks, and economics.

☻ ☻ ☻ EXPLORATION: My Travels

Use the blank map of the United States to mark each state you have traveled to. Count how many states you have seen. If you have not visited a lot of places, you might want to include your whole family, extended family, or friends. Take a poll to find out where they have been and then add them to your map. You might even choose a color coding system to indicate which person visited.

☺ ☻ ☻ EXPLORATION: Penpal

Begin writing to a penpal from another state. You can usually find penpals quickly and easily by searching for homeschool groups on social media and requesting a penpal. Be sure you trust the contact or don't give any personal information. The easiest way to do this is through an e-mail account rather than using a physical address. Make sure to teach your kids ahead of time what kind of information is appropriate to share in an online setting.

Penpals can tell each other about what it is like to live where they do, what neat things they see, and what the climate is like. A kid who lives in Orlando will have a whole different experience than a kid from a rural town in Idaho. A kid from Arizona would be likely experience different things than a kid in Minnesota. When choosing a penpal, try to find one that would likely have a unique lifestyle from your own.

☺ ☻ ☻ EXPLORATION: State Collections

Try to collect a post card from each of the fifty states. You can do this by visiting as many states as possible, writing to agencies within the state who are willing to send you one, or creating a network on social media of people who are willing to send them. Many online homeschooling groups participate in exchanges like this from time to time, and you can even start your own exchange.

You might also like to begin a collection of state quarters. The United States Mint created a quarter for each state and added

them into circulation in the order that the state ratified the Constitution or was admitted into the union. You can collect all fifty of them by just watching for them over time. You might even ask your friends and family to help you watch for the ones you need.

Writer's Workshop

This would be a perfect time to start a states book. You can use a spiral notebook, a bound sketchbook, or bind your own book at a copy center or by sewing the pages together. Make sure to have at least fifty pages (one for each state). As you learn about each state throughout the school year, create a page for it in your book. Include a map, the flag, neat landmarks to see there, the date it became a state, and its nickname. You can include other interesting information you find as well. Illustrate it and keep the book for others to read when you're finished. During this unit you should design the cover. You might also want to make a teaser page with fun facts about some of the states.

On The Web

You might enjoy the *How The States Got Their Shapes* series on YouTube as you begin your study of the United States.

https://www.youtube.com/playlist?list=PLaT-T1rjvNIt5b8EAz-4w2a8cr1ijOEjC4X

SCIENCE: HEAT & TEMPERATURE

On the Web

For high school students, this video from Mr. Anderson explains heat in scientific terms: https://www.youtube.com/watch?v=ldMcDvm29eA.

And this one explains how heat is transfered:

https://www.youtube.com/watch?v=OBVb-V5dpCCA.

Memorization Station

Conduction is when heat moves through a solid object or between solid objects through contact.

Convection is the flow of heat through a fluid (a liquid or gas).

Radiation is the movement of heat through space, without a medium. A light bulb and the sun both use radiation.

Fabulous Fact

Scientists have tried to discover the temperature at which molecules stop moving altogether. They call this absolute zero. So far nothing has ever been brought quite down to absolute zero, though in a lab, conditions have come close.

There is always at least some energy in every body. Energy can be observed on an atomic scale by the movement, or vibration of atoms. Atoms are always moving. Even in outer space molecules move a little, though much more slowly than in warmer places. Atoms with higher energy are moving faster than atoms with lower energy. Energy is always trying to move from high energy areas to low energy areas. When energy moves or transfers from one body to another we call this heat. Heat can transfer through convection, conduction, or radiation.

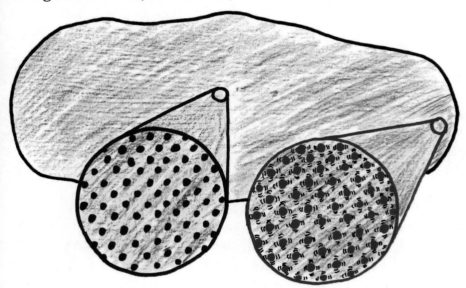

This is a potato that has been in the oven cooking for twenty minutes or so. The outside of the potato (red) is beginning to get very hot, but the center (blue) is still cold. As the potato molecules heat they vibrate faster and faster. The cold molecules are vibrating too, but not nearly so fast.

Heat usually makes matter expand as it increases. The molecules in a solid, like steel, expand more and more as it warms, then at a certain point the molecules get spread enough and warm enough that they begin to turn to liquid. If molecules continue to heat, they can spread even further apart and turn into gas. The temperature at which different substances change states depends on the substance. Not every substance exists in all three states though, some things burn instead of melting or becoming a gas.

Temperature is a measurement of the movement of molecules. There are several different temperature scales. The Fahrenheit scale is based on the temperature at which brine (salt) water freezes, which is represented by 0° on the Fahrenheit scale. The Celsius scale is based on the freezing and boiling points of pure water, 0 and 100 degrees respectively. The Celsius scale has much larger range between one degree and the next and when speaking of everyday temperatures decimals are often necessary for precision. The Kelvin scale is based on absolute zero and has no negative temperatures; it has the same intervals between degrees as the Celsius scale. Scientists use Celsius or Kelvin, but never Fahrenheit. Americans are almost the only people left who regularly use the Fahrenheit scale.

Famous Folks

James Clerk Maxwell wrote *Theory of Heat* in 1871, defining heat and setting off the study of thermodynamics. He is considered the third greatest physicist to ever live, behind Newton and Einstein.

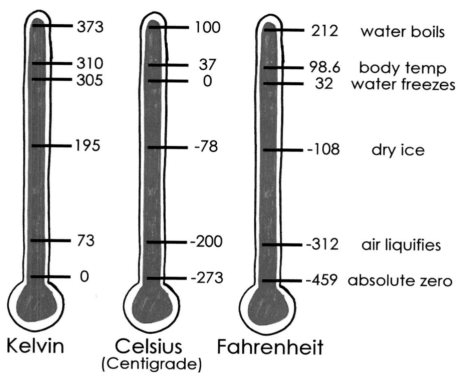

These thermometers show the comparisons between the Kelvin, Celsius, and Fahrenheit scales.

☺ ☻ EXPLORATION: Temperature Conversions

Sometimes it is necessary to convert a temperature from one scale to another. For example, you might be given a temperature in Fahrenheit, but asked to do calculations in Celsius.

To convert Kelvin to Celsius just subtract 273. To convert Celsius to Kelvin add 273. (It's actually -273.15°C, but we'll round.)

To convert between Celsius and Fahrenheit you need a formula:

$$°F = °C \times 1.8 + 32$$

At zero degrees Celsius the temperature is 32 degrees Fahrenheit and so we add 32. But the intervals between degrees is also different in the two scales. A Fahrenheit degree is 1.8 times bigger than a Celsius degree so we also have to multiply by 1.8.

On the Web

Here is a video about temperature from Mr. Anderson: https://www.youtube.com/watch?v=B6hAwZH2m-mA .

On the Web

This video from Khan Academy explains how to convert between Celsius and Fahrenheit. https://www.youtube.com/watch?v=p7TtcisPQN4

Sal uses the relationship between Celsius and Fahrenheit as 9/5, which is the same as 1.8, the value we use.

Famous Folks

The temperature scales are each named after their creators.

Daniel Gabriel Fahrenheit was a physicist and glass blower who lived in the Netherlands. Besides inventing the scale that is named after him, he also invented the glass mercury-filled thermometer.

Anders Celsius was a Swedish astronomer and physicist.

William Thomson, 1st Baron Kelvin, was a British physicist and engineer who determined the value of absolute zero. The scale that begins with absolute zero was named in his honor.

Lord Kelvin, Anders Celsius

Fabulous Fact

A degree symbol is always used when writing temperatures in Celsius or Fahrenheit, but never when writing temperatures in Kelvin.

These are the correct forms:

0°C 32°F 273K

Here is an example:

Your friend from Canada just told you that it's 26 degrees at her house. You think, "Wow, that's awfully cold for June." Then you remember that in Canada they use the Celsius scale. You want to know what 26 degrees is in Fahrenheit. You can use the formula above. In front of the °C you write 26.

$$°F = 26°C \times 1.8 + 32$$

Now you multiply 26 by 1.8 and add 32. You find out it is about 79 °F, a warm spring day.

Now let's say that you are living in London and you use the Celsius scale in your daily life. You are watching the American news and find out that it is 15 degrees in New York City. That seems pretty warm for January, but then you remember that Americans use the Fahrenheit scale.

$$15°F = °C \times 1.8 + 32$$

This time you have to pull out your algebra skills. First you will subtract 32 from both sides of the equation. Then you divide both sides of the equation by 1.8. So you will type 15 - 32 ÷ 1.8 into your calculator. You find out that the temperature in New York is -9.4 °C, well below freezing.

Now, what if you have to convert a Kelvin temperature to a Fahrenheit temperature? Just convert from Kelvin to Celsius and then from Celsius to Fahrenheit.

Create a worksheet for another student with six to ten temperatures in a mixture of Kelvin, Celsius, and Fahrenheit along with the scale to convert to. Swap papers and do the conversions. Round answers to the nearest whole degree. Now swap back and check the answers.

1. Convert 46°F to °C
   46°F = °C × 1.8 + 32
   -32   1.8   -32
   1.8
        8°C
2. Convert 7562 K to °C
   7562 - 273
   7289°C
3. Convert 42K to °F
   42 - 273   °F = -231 × 1.8 + 32
   -231°C   -384°F

☻ ☻ ☻ EXPERIMENT: Latent Heat

As a substance changes from one state to another, like from solid to liquid, the temperature will not rise as long as the transfer is underway. Try this out with a high temperature thermometer and a pan of water.

1. Place a pan about half full of water on the stove.
2. Set a high temperature thermometer (you can use a scientific thermometer or a candy thermometer). It will work best if you can clip the thermometer to the side of the pan or attach it to a clamp to hang halfway into the pot rather than sitting on the bottom of the pot.
3. Turn the heat to high and watch the thermometer as the temperature rises. Record the temperature every thirty seconds on a table, for ten minutes total.
4. Graph the temperature on a piece of graph paper.

The temperature should flatten out as you reach the boiling point. The exact boiling point will depend on your elevation. Places with high elevation boil at lower temperatures because there is less air pressure, so molecules can leave the main body of liquid more easily. The stove continues to transfer heat into the pot of water, but the new energy is used changing the water molecule from liquid to vapor instead of making the molecules move more quickly.

☻ ☻ EXPERIMENT: Pressure Affects Temperature

As a fluid, liquid or gas, is put under pressure it produces heat, as the molecules vibrate faster and faster against one another. If left to sit, the extra heat will dissipate as the system reaches equilibrium, but if the pressure is suddenly released the temperature of the fluid will drop, quickly becoming quite a bit cooler than the surrounding air temperature.

Get a can of aerosol spray. Squeeze the valve and feel the temperature of the aerosol as it is released. It should feel quite a bit cooler than the surrounding air temperature. The liquid gives away energy to the surrounding air as it is depressurized.

☻ ☻ ☻ EXPERIMENT: Volume Changes With Temperature

This experiment can be done with all ages, but other than the measuring of the diameter of the balloon, you can leave the math stuff at the end to the big kids.

You'll need two large containers of water, one cold and one warm, and a blown up balloon.

1. Blow up a balloon (choose a round one) and measure its diameter by setting it against a wall, placing a ruler on top of

Additional Layer

Latent heat is what cools you as you sweat. As the water on your body evaporates in the air, the water absorbs heat from your body. Refrigeration and air conditioners work the same way. Find out more.

Additional Layer

Think about how important measurements are to science and everyday life. Imagine how things would be different if thermometers and temperature scales had never been invented. What other concepts or inventions depend on the ability to accurately measure temperature?

Additional Layer

Though thermometers very like the one first invented by Daniel Fahrenheit are still sold and used on a daily basis around the world, some thermometers have gone very high tech.

This thermometer uses a laser to detect temperature. Learn more.

Fabulous Fact

An ideal gas is one where it is assumed the molecules take no space and it is assumed that there are no forces at work between the molecules; they are unhindered in their flitting about.

This isn't actually quite true in real life, but the equations work out to be close enough for everyday work, which is awfully, awfully close. We almost always assume that gases are ideal. We're going to assume that the gas inside your balloon is also ideal.

Writer's Workshop

Imagine a scenario where a hero (or villain) needs to know the exact pressure inside a balloon. Write about it and describe how she finds the volume.

Additional Layer

If you are concerned with measuring the volume of your balloon more accurately you have to use the water displacement method. Here are instructions on how to do that:

http://science.wonder-howto.com/how-to/measure-volume-balloon-357475/.

the balloon and perpendicular to the wall with one end resting against the wall, and then using another ruler to measure from the surface the balloon rests on to the ruler perpendicular to the wall in centimeters. Take note of the temperature of the air in the room in Celsius. Then convert your temperature to Kelvin by adding 273 (do this every time you take a temperature).

2. Hold the balloon down in a container of cold ice water for about a minute and a half. Measure the diameter of the balloon again in centimeters. Also take note of the temperature of the water in Celsius.
3. Allow the balloon to come to room temperature again.
4. Hold the balloon down in a container of very warm water, but not so hot it will burn, for about 90 seconds. The water we used was very hot tap water; we needed to use kitchen implements to hold the balloon down under water because the water burned our hands. Measure the diameter of the balloon again in centimeters. Take note of the temperature of

the water in Celsius.

5. Discussion: What happened when the balloon got colder? What happened when it got warmer? Why?

Heating the balloon made the molecules inside more energetic. They began to hit the insides of the container (the balloon) more often, making the balloon get a little bigger. Cooling the balloon down made the molecules less energetic, so they hit the insides of the balloon less often, making the balloon get a little smaller. Heat is a form of energy. Adding heat adds energy. Removing heat removes energy.

6. Now find the volume of the balloon at each temperature. Assume the balloon is a sphere, even though it won't be quite spherical; we're fudging a bit. Use this formula to find the volume of a sphere: $V = 4/3 \pi r3$

r is the radius, which you can find by dividing the diameter in half.

How are the volume and temperature related? Do this equation to see if the volume and temperature really are directly proportional. But first change your Celsius temperatures into Kelvin by adding 273 to whatever your Celsius temperatures were.

$$\frac{V1}{T1} = \frac{V2}{T2}$$

The volume of your balloon at first (room temperature) divided by the temperature of your balloon at first, equals the second volume (a cold balloon) divided by the second temperature. Theoretically they should come out equal. Yours will be off a bit, but they'll be close. It doesn't quite work because your balloon system isn't fool proof. The measuring tools you're using are primitive and introduce lots of human error. And your balloon isn't really exactly spherical.

Now do the math comparing the room temperature balloon to the hot balloon. Your answers should come out fairly close.

☺ EXPLORATION: Ideal Gas Law
The Ideal Gas Law says that as pressure and volume in a system (like inside your balloon from the previous experiment) change, so does the temperature.

The formula looks like this:

$$PV = nRT$$

Additional Layer

Calories and BTUs (British Thermal Units) are both common ways of measuring the relationship between heat and temperature.

A calorie is the amount of heat required to raise 1 gram of water 1 degree Celsius.

A BTU is the amount of heat needed to raise 1 pound of water 1 degree Fahrenheit.

Additional Layer

Calories are helpful if we are measuring heat added to water. What if you are adding heat to aluminum or to mercury? We can measure specific heat. Specific heat also helps us compare the energy capacity of various substances to water.

Specific heat is the heat needed to raise 1 gram of any substance 1 degree.

Here is a video that explains how to work problems in specific heat.

https://www.youtube.com/watch?v=eIBVim-dYnDI.

Here you can practice some specific heat problems: http://www.algebralab.org/practice/practice.aspx?file=algebra_specificheatcapacity.xml.

On the Web

This video from Mr. Anderson explains the ideal gas law further: https://youtu.be/ir64EcRkf5Q.

And from Khan Academy: http://www.khanacademy.org/science/chemistry/ideal-gas-laws/v/ideal-gas-equation--pv-nrt.

If you continue on to the rest of the videos on the Khan Academy site you will learn to do ideal gas equations as well.

Famous Folks

The ideal gas law is a synthesis of Boyle's law, Charles's law, and Avogadro's law. The ideal gas law was first used and described by Benoît Paul Émile Clapeyron, a French physicist and pioneer in thermodynamics. Besides developing the ideal gas law, he defined the second law of thermodynamics.

P is the pressure, V is the volume, n is the amount of stuff or moles of gas, R is the ideal constant and T is the temperature.

The constant is, well, constant. It doesn't change as long as we're talking about an ideal gas. But it does change if you change the units you're using. If we speak in Celsius instead of Kelvin we'll get different numbers, for example. We will use temperature in Kelvin, liters for volume, and atmospheres for pressure. If you use these units then the constant, R, equals .082.

$$R = .082$$

What it means is that if the temperature or pressure or volume change then that constant number is how much the rest of the system will change by as well. If the temperature goes up one R, then the volume will go up one R, and so on.

Use the ideal gas equation to find the missing data from the table below (rewrite the table on a chalkboard or paper):

Pressure (atm)	Volume (l)	n (moles)	Temperature (K)
2	2		303
2		.5	341
	4	2	300
3	41	1.5	
4	55		632

Answers: a) .16 mol; b) 7.0 l; c) 12.32 atm; d)1000 K; e) 4.24 mol

You can practice more ideal gas law problems here: http://science.widener.edu/svb/tutorial/idealgascsn7.html. Remember to pay attention to units used. The .0821 R value is only valid for the units explained above. You may need to convert units (like C to K or ml to L) or look up a different R value (like if they use torr to measure pressure rather than atm).

☺ ☻ EXPERIMENT: Energy Changes

Remember temperature is one way to measure how much average energy is in a system. So we can use temperature to observe whether energy levels are changed. Use a thermometer to measure the temperature in your hand. Hold the thermometer tightly in your hand and record the temperature after the thermometer has quit climbing. Now rub your hands briskly together for a minute. Take the temperature of your hands again. Was energy added to your hands? Yes, you can tell because the temperature increased.

In this case you increased the temperature of your hands through mechanical energy. What other types of energy can increase the temperature and energy in a system?

☺ ☻ EXPERIMENT: Conducting Heat

To conduct is to transfer heat from one substance to another by touching. Some things conduct heat better than others. You can feel the difference if you step out of the shower onto a slick tile floor versus stepping out onto a cushy bath mat. A good conductor allows heat to move quickly and a poor conductor moves heat slowly. Which is a better conductor - the tile floor or the bath mat? What do you predict would be a better conductor of heat - water or air?

Place two identical containers into the fridge, one should be filled with air (empty), the other should be filled with water. Place a thermometer into each one. Let it sit inside the fridge for several hours to cool completely (an adult can set this up the night before if you wish). The two systems should be at the same temperature. Check to be sure they are. Now blindfold one person. Take the two containers out of the fridge and place the person's right hand into the water and their left into the air. Have them tell you which is colder. Test again with more than one person.

The system that felt colder would be the better heat conductor. When something feels cold that means heat is being conducted away from your body.

☺ ☻ EXPERIMENT: Convection

Heat transferred through a fluid, liquid or gas, happens by random Brownian motion. And as more heat is applied to a liquid or gas, more molecular motion is happening too, transferring the heat more rapidly. If you get a big movement of heat, you can get it to flow, like an ocean current; this is called advection.

You can watch an advection current in action with this simple experiment.

1. Fill a small cup with hot water. Place in a couple of drops of red food coloring and cover tightly the aluminum foil.
2. Place the cup in a larger clear container, at least twice as tall as the smaller cup. A glass pitcher or vase would work well.
3. Now pour cold water into the large container until it is nearly full.
4. Poke a hole into the foil of the cup.
5. The hot colored water will flow through the cooler water in a stream.

Additional Layer

Make a mind map with these words from this unit:

temperature

convection

Celsius

Kelvin

absolute zero

heat

energy

thermometer

Fahrenheit

conduction

radiation

A mind map is a way to organize information so it is easier to recall. Here are an examples of mind maps: http://www.mindmapping.com/.

There is no right or wrong way to organize a mind map; it should be organized in a way that makes sense to the creator.

Using colors and simple illustrations can make a mind map more fun and useful for the creator too.

Additional Layer

Convection is a major force in all weather patterns from hurricanes to a sea breeze to jet streams to ocean currents.

Fabulous Fact

Brownian motion happens when molecules randomly move around. This only happens in fluids, not in solids.

Fabulous Facts

Thermodynamics is the study of heat and temperature and how they behave. There are some laws regarding thermodynamics that have been discovered. (Clicking on the links will take you to videos by Mr. Anderson.)

1. Energy cannot be created or destroyed; it can only be transfered from one system to another.

https://youtu.be/qVAvmieRM1E

2. Systems and the entire universe are tending toward a state of entropy (lower forms of energy, more disorder).

https://youtu.be/Yoek-FxOizj4

3. The entropy of a system approaches zero as temperatures approach absolute zero. This is because as molecules lose heat they slow down and perfect order is possible. But no system can ever actually reach absolute zero or zero entropy.

Which direction does the hot water flow? Why? Hot water is less dense than cold water.

Eventually the hot water and cooler water will completely combine as the heat is convected through Brownian motion.

☺ ☺ ☺ EXPERIMENT: Convection Currents

You can make your own visible convection currents that resemble the ones on the surface of the sun using just a pie tin, water with food coloring, and a bit of dish soap. Fill the pie tin about halfway full of water and place it over a hot plate or stove. Add 2 Tbsp. dish soap and mix it in carefully and slowly so it doesn't bubble or foam up. Add a few drops of food coloring and mix it in carefully as well. Now turn on the heat to the lowest setting and observe the visible currents that form in the liquid as it heats up.

Mixing the water well at the beginning created a uniformly dense solution. As the pan is heated the liquid on the bottom heats up first. As things increase in temperature they become less dense, so that liquid on the bottom is becoming not only hotter, but also less dense. This lighter liquid is then pushed upward through the denser, cooler liquid which settles on the bottom.

The small region where you see the rising and sinking fluid is called a convection cell. The food coloring doesn't do anything in the experiment except making the movement within the convection cell a little more visible.

Tip: If the experiment doesn't seem to be working, try another brand of dish soap. Some work better than others.

☺ ☺ ☺ EXPERIMENT: Radiation
Energy can also be transferred through radiation. This is how the sun heats the earth. The sun doesn't touch the earth, but the heat is transferred through a vacuum (space) to the surface of the earth.

You can observe how different surfaces absorb heat differently depending on their color and texture. Place each of these objects outside in direct sunlight and test how their temperatures are different after five minute time intervals, checking for thirty minutes.

- Cardboard covered with smooth, shiny aluminum foil
- Cardboard painted matte black
- Cardboard painted gloss black
- Cardboard painted white
- Cardboard left plain
- Cardboard painted blue or green

Before you begin have each child predict how they think the temperature of each will be affected. Will some be hotter, cooler, the same? Which ones?

☺ ☺ ☺ EXPLORATION: Heat Transfer
Go visit http://www.pbslearningmedia.org/asset/lsps07_int_heattransfer/ to see an interactive that explains and gives everyday examples of radiation, conduction, and convection. Then go visit http://d3tt741pwxqwm0.cloudfront.net/WGBH/conv16/conv16-int-thermalenergy/index.html#/ for an even deeper look at thermal energy transfer.

Additional Layer
Convection currents aren't just for science experiments. They occur in all kinds of liquids from the ocean to your cup of hot cocoa.

Our atmosphere is full of convection currents that affect the weather we're having.

The surface of the sun has thousands of convection currents, some bigger than our entire planet.

At the center of the earth, the core has churning convection currents that create the magnetic field that makes our compasses work. Earthquakes are also a result of convection currents within the earth's mantle.

Lava lamps also have convection currents.

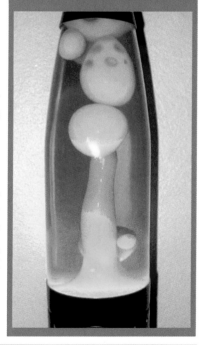

THE ARTS: PATRIOTIC MUSIC

The Battle Hymn of the Republic was written by Julia Ward Howe, the wife of an abolitionist during the Civil War. She had been visiting the Union army's encampment near Washington D.C. on the Potomac River when she wrote the famous hymn.

Writer's Workshop

While you're listening to the music from this unit, have kids listen, write, and draw. They can write about or draw some of their favorite things about America.

Patriotic music has an amazing capacity to stir our souls. Music is a very special kind of art. It can set a mood, inspire a message, and help us to relate to people, stories, and situations. America's patriotic music has helped fill enlistment ranks, inspired our fighting forces, made us well up with tears at hometown parades, and kindled a love of country.

What is patriotism? Patriotism is loyalty and an attachment to a nation. It is pride in the cultural, historical, ethnic, and political stories of a nation. Patriotic music tells these stories. The patriotic music of America includes messages about its origins, its flag, its military endeavors, and its beautiful landscape.

Patriotism is critical to the success of a nation because people who feel this connection to their country are willing to give what it takes to help it be great. Patriots are willing to do more for their communities and societies. They are willing to be fair and honest in business dealings even if it costs them something. They are willing to serve in public office and resist the tendency to corruption that comes with that power. They are willing to lay down their lives for the ideals of the country and go to war to protect it. No country is perfect, but patriotism contributes to the greatness of a nation because the individual actions of patriots add up.

U.S. Navy photo by Mass Communication Specialist 2nd Class Chelsea Radford [Public domain], via Wikimedia Commons

Patriotic music has long been an important part of the United States of America, rooting back to the colonial period before the birth of the country. Many, many versions have been made of the songs we'll be exploring in this unit. Hopefully you'll spend a good portion of this unit just listening to many different versions, paying attention to the lyrics, learning the songs, and discussing their meanings. Beyond that, take some time to discuss these questions:

- What is patriotism?
- What is a patriot?
- Can you feel patriotism

even when there are bad things happening in your nation?
- What do national heroes have to do with patriotism?
- Is patriotism just blind nationalism?
- Could a truly patriotic person challenge the wrongdoing of a government?
- What role does music play in patriotism?
- Is patriotic music really just propaganda?
- Is patriotism always good? Can it be used for evil, ill will, or commercialism?
- Why does so much patriotic music have to do with war?

☺ ☺ ☺ EXPLORATION: The Liberty Song

The Liberty Song was one of America's first patriotic songs. The lyrics to *The Liberty Song* were written by John Dickinson, one of America's founders and also a member of the Continental Congress.

One of the verses goes like this:

> *Then join hand in hand, brave Americans all,*
> *By uniting we stand, by dividing we fall;*
> *In so righteous a cause let us hope to succeed,*
> *For heaven approves of each generous deed.*

This was the first recorded mention of the sentiment "United we stand, divided we fall" that has become an important concept to Americans. Have a discussion about how it is even possible for such a diverse nation to be united. In what ways can we be united? Are there things that divide us? Do we all need to believe the same things to be united? Consider the questions several ways - as individuals, as communities, as states, as a cultural group, and as a political nation as a whole. Finally, what do you think the righteous cause was that Dickinson was referring to?

☺ ☺ ☺ EXPLORATION: Chester

Chester was sung during the American Revolution. No one is sure why William Billings, the song's composer, called it *Chester*. It could have been named for the town of Chester, or it could be referencing the meaning of the name Chester ("camp of soldiers"), or perhaps he had some other reason entirely.

These are the some of the words:

> *Let tyrants shake their iron rod,*
> *And slavery clank her galling chains,*
> *We'll fear them not, we'll trust in God;*
> *New England's God forever reigns.*

Teaching Tips

If you just want to teach kids some songs, carry on. But if you want to really teach your kids to sing, you might like these tips from a professional https://www.youtube.com/watch?v=nkQY-JHX2b3k&list=PLDB-C881803018D089.

Famous Folks

Irving Berlin wrote *God Bless America*. It's neat that he was an immigrant from Siberia. He also donated all the royalties to the Boy Scouts and Girl Scouts of America.

Famous Folks

Francis Scott Key was an attorney. He handled many high profile cases and eventually became the U.S. Attorney General. When the British seized Dr. William Beanes during the War of 1812, Key was sent to arrange for his release. It was that night as he sat on a nearby ship, held by the British because he was a witness to their strategic position during the Battle of Baltimore, that he wrote *The Star Spangled Banner*.

Expedition

Attend an event that includes a flag ceremony and singing of the national anthem. Use proper flag etiquette and pay attention to the words of the song as you listen or sing it.

The foe comes on with haughty stride,
Our troops advance with martial noise;
Their veterans flee before our arms.
And generals yield to beardless boys.

Orchestra New England performed it in traditional attire with a pipe organ. You can see it here: https://youtu.be/RxhRXHtX4pg

It is known as our first national anthem. William Billings published it in the very first published book of American music, *The New England Psalm Singer,* with a cover that was engraved by his good friend, Paul Revere. He went on to teach music classes, open America's first singing school, and organize the first church choir in America.

☺ ☺ ☺ EXPLORATION: Star Spangled Banner Story

The Star Spangled Banner is the national anthem of the United States of America. It was written by Francis Scott Key and is about the flag.

The American flag is technically called the "Flag of the United States of America," but it has a lot of other nicknames: Stars and Stripes; Old Glory; the Red, White, and Blue; and the Star Spangled Banner. It has 13 stripes that represent the original 13 colonies and 50 stars that represent each of the 50 states. We are currently using the 27th version of the flag. Stars have been added each time new states are included (1959 was the last update when Hawaii became a state). The current flag was designed by a high school student. Robert G. Heft was a 17-year-old student from Ohio who was given a school assignment to design the 50 star flag. He only got a B- on his project, but he submitted it anyway, and his design was chosen and accepted by Congress. His teacher changed his grade to an A.

There is a neat story behind the National Anthem too. It goes all the way back to the War of 1812. Watch this video to learn the story behind *The Star Spangled Banner*:

https://www.youtube.com/watch?v=6hZe8CPGA1E

Make a storyboard of the story after you watch the video. Illustrate and write about the major points of the story. You'll find a storyboard printable at the end of this unit.

☺ ☺ ☻ EXPLORATION: America The Beautiful

America the Beautiful began as a poem, not intended to be a song at all.

In 1893 Katherine Lee Bates, an English professor, took a train ride across the United States from Massachusetts to Colorado. She passed through the central plains and then on to the Rocky Mountains. While at Pike's Peak the words to the poem began to come to her and she wrote them down.

Her poem was later published. It was put to the music of a hymn written by Samuel A. Ward in 1910, and we are still singing it today. Learn to sing the song in parts using helps from this website:

http://calebhugo.com/how-to-sing-harmony/america-the-beautiful/.

It has the music for each part separated out so you can hear just the notes you are supposed to sing.

Write your own poem about beautiful things you've seen in America. What are your favorite places? What makes America beautiful to you? Either illustrate your poem or pair it with photographs of America.

☺ ☻ EXPLORATION: March 2, 3, 4

John Phillip Sousa was a famous Navy Band leader and composer. He is best known for his military style march music, and especially for writing the song *The Stars and Stripes Forever*.

Go on a webquest at the Marine Band website and read the article about John Philip Sousa:

http://www.marineband.marines.mil/About/OurHistory/JohnPhilipSousa.aspx

Find the answers to each of the following questions in the article.

- What was John Philip Sousa's title?
- Which instrument did John love playing most of all?
- In 1880 he received a special telegram. What was it about?

On The Web

Watch this version of *The Star Spangled Banner* sung by Whitney Houston at the 1991 Super Bowl, hailed as one of the most memorable patriotic moments.

https://youtu.be/N_lCmBvYMRs

Additional Layer

The Power of Patriotism by Delynn Decker tells the story of Francis Scott Key. It is colorful and fun and told in story form, but still has a lot of great facts that kids will enjoy. It would be a great read to go along with this unit.

Teaching Tip

To help you memorize the words to the songs you learn during this unit, pass a ball around a circle of people. Randomly pause the music and see if the person holding the ball can say the next line in the song. If they do, they stay in the circle. If they don't know, they are out. Continue passing and playing until you have a winner.

Vocabulary

spacious: large, vast

amber: golden or yellow-orange colored

grain: edible seeds of grasses like wheat, corn, and oats

majesties: grand, regal, dignified (often used for royalty)

plain: a large area of flat land with few trees

brotherhood: a community of people linked by common interests

Writer's Workshop

Create a series of postcards of scenes from America as you learn about patriotic music. You could show a variety of scenes from landmarks and big cities to national parks and landscapes. Write about America on the cards.

On The Web

Listen to The President's Own U.S. Marine Band playing *The Stars and Stripes Forever*.

https://youtu.be/a-7XWhyvIpE

Can you identify all of the instruments being played?

Listen to some other versions as well.

- Sousa was both a strict band leader and a talented composer. He is also known for having the Marine Band make its first what?
- The Marine Band began the tradition of its annual tour (except in times of war) with permission from which President of the United States?
- Where was Sousa's final Navy Band concert given?
- What is the Sousa Baton?
- Which of Sousa's songs is the national march?

America, I see your lakes, your rivers, streams and seas.
I see the glory of your heights, the hills and mounts I've climbed.
I love to travel down below to valleys, caves, and falls.
From glowing city to deep, green woods, your beauty is divine.

Once you've found all of the answers, listen to some of John Philip Sousa's marches. March along to them around the room while keeping the beat with your feet.

☺ ☺ ☺ EXPLORATION: Military Anthems

Play a guessing game. Use YouTube to play clips of each of the military anthems and guess which branch of the military uses the song. If you'd like a little bit of history to go along with each song as it is guessed, you can download this pdf that describes each one: http://www.wnymoaa.org/service%20songs%20and%20history.pdf

Use these anthems:

- Marine Corps Anthem: The United States Marine Corps Hymn
- Air Force Anthem: The U.S. Air Force (aka Wild Blue Yonder)
- Army Anthem: The Army Goes Rolling Along
- Navy Anthem: Anchors Aweigh
- Coast Guard Anthem: Semper Paratus

Arrange to talk with a veteran about his or her experiences in the military and the significance of the military anthem from the branch they served in. Prepare thoughtful questions to ask ahead of time about the military, patriotism, and personal experiences the person has had.

☺ ☺ ☺ EXPLORATION: George M. Cohan

Patriotic music continued on in popularity in America through the World Wars and beyond. George Cohan was born on July 4th, 1878 and seemed to be born to sing and dance. He wrote three very famous tunes that would have been familiar to all Americans during the World Wars era - *You're A Grand Old Flag, Yankee Doodle Boy*, and *Over There*. Not only did he write music, but he also performed on the stage. He began in Vaudeville and eventually on the big Broadway Stage at Times Square. He made a career out of patriotic music and shows. He loved musical theater and especially comedic musical theater. In all, he wrote over 500 songs, although he was musically untrained.

See him on the stage and learn about him by watching this PBS segment all about George M. Cohan called "All The Gang At 42nd Street." https://youtu.be/CeDDqYrfvt8

☺ ☺ EXPLORATION: Keep the Beat

Most of the patriotic songs we enjoy have a strong and steady beat. *Yankee Doodle, You're A Grand Old Flag*, and *This Land*

Additional Layer

Do you play an instrument? Go visit Making-MusicFun.net to get lots of cool free printable sheet music. First, select your instrument and then look at the index of songs. They have Yankee Doodle, The Star Spangled Banner, and lots of others.

http://makingmusicfun. net/htm/printit_free_ printable_sheet_music_ index.htm

---

Famous Folks

George M. Cohan is the only actor to have his statue in Times Square. He was also awarded the Congressional Gold Medal by President Roosevelt for boosting morale during World War I.

Additional Layer

Most American patriotic music stems from wars and military endeavors, but there is another kind of patriotic music that simply celebrates the features or heroes of a country. Learn some of these songs as well to see a different side of patriotism:

Erie Canal
John Henry
Home on the Range
Roll on Columbia
This Land Is My Land

Teaching Tip

Rhythm sticks would be a great addition to the "Keep the Beat" Exploration. Just cut 1 inch wood dowels into lengths of about 8 inches. Give each kid two sticks and let them hit them together or on the ground, on their laps, or on homemade drums (bowls, pots, pans, and coffee cans) to keep the beat with.

Additional Layer

Contra dancing is a form of folk dancing that was very popular in the late 1700's America up until the present. In contra dance long lines of couples typically form up in sets. They move according to whatever a caller calls out. Partners stand opposite, or contra, to each other.

You can find contra dancing groups just about anywhere. These gatherings are generally family friendly and alcohol free so consider taking your family.

Before you go, you might want to learn some moves: https://youtu. be/J4xvqmD64eg.

is My Land are all great choices for this exploration. Choose one of these songs to learn to sing. Once you know it well, play some rhythm games while singing.

Begin by playing a clapping game. Sit in a circle and choose a clap leader. The leader will find a rhythm within the song and begin clapping it to the beat in a pattern. To make the pattern they can use slaps on their knees and claps with the hands. Keep going as everyone finds the beat and pattern and joins in. Once everyone has got it down together, choose a new clap leader who will make a new pattern. Continue until everyone has had a chance to be the clap leader.

For the second game get everyone a tennis ball and try to bounce the tennis ball to the beat of each song. You can try it with playground balls, basketballs, or racquetballs too.

For the final game, move to the rhythm of the music. You can do free movement around an open area or do it follow the leader style. In all of your movements, consider the music and keep the beat with your body.

☻ ☻ ☻ EXPLORATION: Yankee Doodle Dancing

Folk dancing has been a long tradition in America. American folk dances borrow from all over the world, because Americans came from all over the world. The styles borrow from a range of dances, everything from dancing around a maypole and Native American dances to Irish jigs and Latin salsas. Try out this patriotic line dance to the tune of *Yankee Doodle Dandy*. https://youtu.be/MdPr8x_mmjs

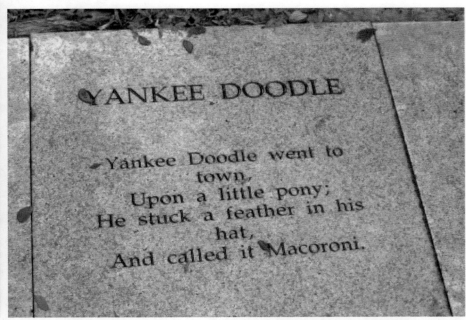

☺ ☺ ☺ **EXPLORATION: Sing Along**

Have a sing-along with family or friends after learning some of the patriotic songs from this unit. Hold it around a campfire, around a piano, or outside at a park. Make sure to have snacks to share -- s'mores or a red, white, and blue fruit platter (blueberries, strawberries and bananas) would be a memorable treat. These are some fun sing-along songs you might enjoy:

- *You're a Grand Old Flag*
- *Yankee Doodle*
- *The Star Spangled Banner*
- *America the Beautiful*
- *My Country 'Tis of Thee*
- *God Bless America*
- *God Bless the USA*
- *This Land is My Land*
- *Home On The Range*

☺ ☺ ☺ **EXPLORATION: Name That Tune**

At the end of this unit, play a game using clips from all the songs you listened to and learned. Play just a short clip and see who can be the first to name the song. Award a bonus point if the kid can tell something he or she learned about it as well. Keep score and announce the winner after all the clips have been played.

Fabulous Fact

My Country 'Tis of Thee was written by Samuel Smith to the tune of Britain's national anthem, *God Save The Queen.*

Other countries have used the same melody including Germany, Switzerland, Norway, Sweden, Iceland, and Liechtenstein.

In fact, before the '96 European Football Championship qualifying match between Northern Ireland and Liechtenstein it was played twice.

When Northern Ireland and England play each other it is only played once.

Coming up next . . .

Unit 4-2

Expanding Nation
Pacific States
Motors & Engines
Tall Tales

My ideas for this unit:

Title: _____ **Topic:** _____

_____

_____

_____

_____

_____

_____

_____

_____

_____

Title: _____ **Topic:** _____

_____

_____

_____

_____

_____

_____

_____

_____

_____

_____

Title: _____ **Topic:** _____

_____

_____

_____

_____

_____

_____

_____

_____

_____

Title: _____   **Topic:** _____

_____

_____

_____

_____

_____

_____

_____

_____

_____

_____

Title: _____   **Topic:** _____

_____

_____

_____

_____

_____

_____

_____

_____

_____

_____

_____

Title: _____   **Topic:** _____

_____

_____

_____

_____

_____

_____

_____

_____

_____

_____

Constitutional Convention

In 1787 delegates from each of the 13 states met in Philadelphia to discuss fixing the Articles of Confederation. They ended up scrapping the Articles and instead writing a new document for the nation called the Constitution of the United States of America. In this picture you can see George Washington standing and speaking to some of the delegates who had voted him president of the Convention.

Timeline Unit 4-I

Summer 1776 <small>4-I</small> Articles of Confederation drafted 	**1781** <small>4-I</small> Articles of Confederation finally ratified 	**Sep 1786** <small>4-I</small> Annapolis Convention of five States meets 	**Summer 1787** <small>4-I</small> Constitutional Convention in Philadelphia 
Sep 17, 1787 <small>4-I</small> Constitution is signed by the delegates 	**June 21, 1788** <small>4-I</small> The Constitution takes effect with the ratification of New Hampshire, the ninth state 	**April 30, 1789** <small>4-I</small> George Washington is sworn in as the First President 	**1791** <small>4-I</small> The Bill of Rights is added to the Constitution 

Communism	**Capitalism**	**Fascism**
Socialism	**Democracy**	**Anarchy**
Absolute Monarchy/ Imperial	**Oligarchy/ Dictatorship**	**Republic**
Constitutional Monarchy	**Mixed Economy**	Ruled by a hereditary king or queen, usually with the help of an aristocracy

Property is owned and administered by individuals who are also responsible for and retain power over their own welfare.	Government controls nearly all economic activity while ostensibly leaving the ownership of property in the hands of the people.	Government provides many services such as health care, education, and welfare by forcibly taking money from citizens to redistribute it to others. In addition, this economic type utilizes government control and regulation in varying degrees to achieve goals of the elite ruling class.
Economies that have parts of two or more types of other economies mixed in.	A state of no government.	A limited monarchy, constrained by a constitution and ruled with the help of an elected legislature.
Majority rules with no protection for the minority.	Absolute rule by a small group, either with an individual or political party in charge. Power is held by force.	A limited government, deriving its power from the people, with a constitution of law restraining the government from taking the liberty of the people.
Ostensibly all property and goods are owned in common and shared equally, but in reality the wealth is held by a few elite and taken from the rest of the people by force. All means of production are owned by the government.		

Cut cards apart and lay face down, except the cards in ALL CAPS.
Match the definitions with the names of economic and government types.
Then place each government and economic type under its major heading. The key is above in this unit (4-1).

This page is last on purpose so you can print it onto a different color of paper if you like. These cards are not part of the game, but are the major headings you place the definitions and terms under.

FREE MARKET

CONTROLLED ECONOMY

LIMITED GOVERNMENT

TOTALITARIAN

ANARCHY

Madison Says . . .

These are all quotes by James Madison. Read them as you cut and paste them onto the previous "Madison Says . . ." page. Do you agree with these ideas?

Knowledge will forever govern ignorance; and a people who mean to be their own governors must arm themselves with the power which knowledge gives.

If men were angels, no government would be necessary.

I believe there are more instances of the abridgement of freedom of the people by gradual and silent encroachments by those in power than by violent and sudden usurpations.

Americans have the right and advantage of being armed - unlike the citizens of other countries whose governments are afraid to trust the people with arms.

The happy Union of these States is a wonder; their Constitution a miracle; their example the hope of Liberty throughout the world.

Do not separate text from historical background. If you do, you will have perverted and subverted the Constitution, which can only end in a distorted . . . form of illegitimate government.

Where an excess of power prevails, property of no sort is duly respected. No man is safe in his opinions, his person, his faculties, or his possessions.

In framing a government which is to be administered by men over men you must first enable the government to control the governed; and in the next place oblige it to control itself.

Judicial	
Legislative	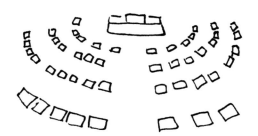
Executive	
Signs or Vetoes Laws Receives Foreign Dignitaries Gives Pardons Executes the Law Commands the Armed Forces	Decides on the Constitutionality of Laws Defends the People From Attacks on the Constitution By Lawmakers or the President
Makes New Laws Declares War Ratifies Treaties Budgets Money Issues Taxes	**Three Branches of the United States Government**

Three Branches by the Constitution

LEGISLATIVE BRANCH
CONGRESS

- Can propose constitutional amendments
- Governs U.S. territories
- Ratifies treaties

HOUSE OF REPRESENTATIVES

Elected by their district for 2 years

SENATE

Elected by their state for 6 years

- Hears cases involving 2 states, foreign nations, federal law, etc.
- Tries all constitutional cases in court
- Makes the tie breaking vote in the senate
- Tries impeached officials
- Proposes bills for raising revenue
- After a bill is passed it is approved or vetoed here
- Lays and collects taxes
- Can borrow money
- Regulate commerce with foreign nations
- Make immigration (naturalization) laws

- Make bankruptcy laws
- Coin and regulate money
- Create standard weights & measures
- Punish counterfeiters

- Establish post office & roads
- Write patent & copyright law
- Establish lower federal courts
- Write maritime law

EXECUTIVE BRANCH

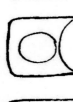 PRESIDENT

Elected by the electoral college for 4 years

→ VICE PRESIDENT

- Appoints ambassadors, judges, officials, etc.
- Approves or denies the president's appointments
- Make treaties
- Can grant pardons
- Commander in chief of the armed froces
- If the electoral college votes tie, they choose the next president
- Counts the electoral college votes and declares the President
- Organize, arm, and call up the militia
- Directly govern the national capital city
- Make laws to execute the powers given the federal govt.

- Receive ambassadors & foreign officials
- Recommend legislation to congress, report on the state of the Union

- Declare war
- Raise and support armies
- Establish a navy

JUDICIAL BRANCH

SUPREME COURT

Appointed by the president, confirmed by the senate for life

Layers of Learning

Checks and Balances in the Constitution

The Constitution was written with human nature in mind, specifically the human tendency to crave power over others. The whole point of a republic is that every one governs him or her self, but human nature tells us that we are not content with that, we must attempt to force our will on others. So as we speak of checks and balances in the Constitution we will speak of them as powers that each entity has over others as each jealously guards its own influence. Then we will speak of how those checks and balances are threatened and the danger of them breaking down.

The Constitution deals with five main entities: The Federal Government consisting of Legislature, Executive, and Judicial branches, the States, and the People. The only entity that is not checked in its power is the People, the People have all the power and grant certain powers to the Federal Government and to the States in which they live.

Federal			States	People
Executive	Legislative	Judicial		All power comes from the people, the people are restrained in their power only by the principles of common law that say 1. Do no injury to others and 2. Do all you have agreed to do.
Federal role is small and defined by the specific powers in the Constitution			States role is larger, but cannot infringe on the Peoples rights and must have a republican form	
Propose Law	Write Law	Builds a body of case law, through precedent, which can be overturned by future courts	Write laws within their state States appoint senators, who can also be recalled by the state.[1]	Vote out people who make bad laws, the People who place officials in office have power over those officials.
Veto laws Upholds the laws written by congress	Override vetoes with 2/3 vote	Determine if the law is unconstitutional[2]	Refuse to observe an unconstitutional law[3]	Sue the federal or state government over unconstitutional laws, petition or demonstrate against unconstitutional laws
			All laws must be uniform	
Appoints federal judges and other officials	Approves Executive federal appointees		Appoints state and local judges	

		Defend citizens from out of control fed or state governments, they have the last say.	Defend their citizens from Federal agents by refusing them access to the state, by suing the federal government.	
	Controls the money, President can do nothing if it is not funded. Can tax the states forcibly.[4]		States must be taxed uniformly.[5]	Individual citizens can not be taxed by the federal government.[6]
Can have a standing army, but it is only funded for two years at a time				Most of the defense depends on armed and trained citizens in a militia[7]
Commander in chief of the armed forces	Sole power to declare war, Power of funding or de-funding war efforts			Right to bear arms and defend themselves against any and all aggressors
Makes, negotiates treaties Receives foreign ambassadors and heads of state	Ratifies all treaties and agreements with foreign nations Can force the states to abide by treaties			Public opinion, especially that expressed through the press and through peaceful assemblies and petitions controls public policy, gets people hired or fired, or impeached, can destroy or build entire agencies.
	Can amend the Constitution with a 2/3 vote in House and Senate		Can amend the Constitution with 2/3 of the states in convention	

1. This was changed by the seventeenth amendment, making senators directly elected by the people of their state. This removes influence over legislation that the states had and makes the states completely unrepresented in the federal government, shifting the power from the states, toward the federal government.

2. The power to determine if a law is unconstitutional, thereby overturning the law for good, is not a power given to the courts in the Constitution, but it is implied by the existence of the court and the Constitution. If the Constitution exists and if the court's job is to uphold the law and protect the People under the law, and the Constitution is the highest law in the land than the court can decide that other, lower laws violate the higher laws and thereby strike down bad laws. This power was first used in 1803 in the Marbury vs. Madison case and has been well established as precedent.

3. This right of the states is a little shaky, as it has never really been used. The right of nullification was first explained by Jefferson during the 1798 Kentucky Resolutions which were written to protest the Alien and Sedition Acts, the first unconstitutional acts written, a mere ten years after the Constitution was established. Jefferson's argument was that since the Constitution is a document delegating certain powers to the federal government, any undelegated act or law is void since the federal

government didn't have the power to create such a law in the first place and any state can declare it void on constitutional grounds within the borders of their state. Since there is no court independent of both the states and the Federal government, there could be no appeal from this by the Federal government.

4. The right to tax the states, but not individuals, is clearly established by the Constitution. The purpose is to protect individual people from the overwhelming force of the Federal government. If the feds decide to go after an individual there is essentially nothing that person can do to protect him or her self. But States are much larger and more powerful than individuals so the Federal government deals with them. However, the sixteenth amendment which allows the direct taxation of individuals changed this. The seventeenth amendment also destroyed the concept of "uniform taxation", which means the law treats everyone the same whether rich or poor, male or female, black or white. Instead we have special rules and loopholes for different groups based on all sorts of external features.

5. The Founders envisioned, and indeed lived in, a country where every adult male was a member of the militia (or paid a tax to be exempt) and the standing army was limited to a small force, which would be trained and prepared to lead the militia in the event of an invasion or domestic insurrection. The idea was that everyone in a republic is responsible for their own safety and therefore must provide for that safety. The other aspect of that is that it is the People who have the military power and not the Federal government. Further, a citizen army is much more reluctant to go to war than a professional army, keeping the country out of unprofitable or unjust wars. Today, that concept is flipped on its head with a large standing army and a general disdain for armed citizens. A hallmark of a republic is a militia; a hallmark of a top-down power hungry government is a large standing army and a disarmed populace.

There are several ways that this system of checks and balances, designed to protect the People and their power, can be undermined.

1. Political Parties: Political parties create alliances across the entities above, instead of within. A Democrat congress will side with a Democrat President instead of with the other members of the legislature in protecting the power of the legislature. Republican citizens will side with a bad law in congress, just because it was a Republican sponsored law, even if it destroys the power of the People themselves. Parties also cause the politicizing of the courts, changing them from entities that understand and protect the law and the People into legislative bodies that "interpret" the Constitution and the law to further their agenda.

2. Heavily Biased Press: People are biased and there's no way around that, but if the balance gets off and the whole body of the press favors one political ideology over another then you have a situation where half the politicians are not held accountable for what they do and the other half are steamrolled in everything they do, regardless of the actual consequences. Ideally the press, which is the voice of the People, would be in the tank for the People and suspicious of government and politicians whatever their stripe. It is the sacred and solemn job of the press to keep the People informed of the truth and to promote the liberty of the People, of which they are a part.

3. Uninformed People: In a republic every citizen is responsible for the government and responsible to protect themselves. If the people are uninformed of government principles, the Constitution, current events, and issues; if the people do not even understand which principles will maintain their liberty, then there is no hope that they will have any liberty. It is a vested interest of the power hungry politicians to have an uneducated public so that the public can be manipulated and the power of the federal government can be increased. Formerly it was always the sole responsibility of the states to ensure public education, this was in part because the states, in desiring to fend off the power of the federal government, do want an educated public.

4. Large Standing Army: As stated above, in a republic the People are supposed to defend themselves, be well armed, and well trained. But this threatens the federal government who then cannot

unilaterally use the armed forces to coerce the People. A weak, unarmed populace coupled with a well trained standing federal army tips the balance of physical power completely toward the Federal government and away from the People. It's all good until the feds decide to use their power to force unconstitutional measures.

5. Bureaucracy: As we increasingly have a massive number of public "servants", almost all of whom serve under the executive branch, we have more and more unelected officials who make rules which have the force of law. The EPA is a great example. You can be deprived of your property and your liberty if you violate a rule made by an unelected EPA official, a rule that never passed through the Congress, a rule that was never signed into law by the president, a rule that was never debated in the press. Expansive executive departments and unelected officials undermine liberty. A republic does not need a bureaucracy to fulfill its constitutional roles, the presence of one indicates how far we have strayed from the Constitution.

6. Personal Immorality: Just as people in a republic must be informed and well-armed, so must they be able to govern themselves. It is an eternal principle that if you can't govern yourself then some-one else will do it for you. If we are a people who have to have our every behavior legislated and controlled then we're not a free people. If we can't be honest without being coerced then we're not free. If we can't be faithful to our families and kind to our children without being coerced than we can't be free. If we can't keep our word and honor our contracts without being forced then we can't have liberty. And it gets worse, an immoral people will attempt to use the law to do immoral things. Just because something is legal doesn't make it right. It was legal to kill Jews, gays, and others in Hitler's Germany, but we can all agree that that didn't make it right or moral.

1st Amendment	**2nd Amendment**	**3rd Amendment**
4th Amendment	**5th Amendment**	**6th Amendment**
7th Amendment	**8th Amendment**	**9th Amendment**
10th Amendment	**No laws about religion, speech, or the press**	**No laws restricting ownership of weapons**

No quartering soldiers in civilian's houses	No searching a person's home, possessions, or person without a warrant	No trying a person twice for the same crime
No delaying trials while holding a person in prison	Crimes must be tried before a jury	No punishing people with cruel or unusual means
People retain all their rights, not just those listed	States and the People have all power not given to the federal government	

The United States of America

The United States of America

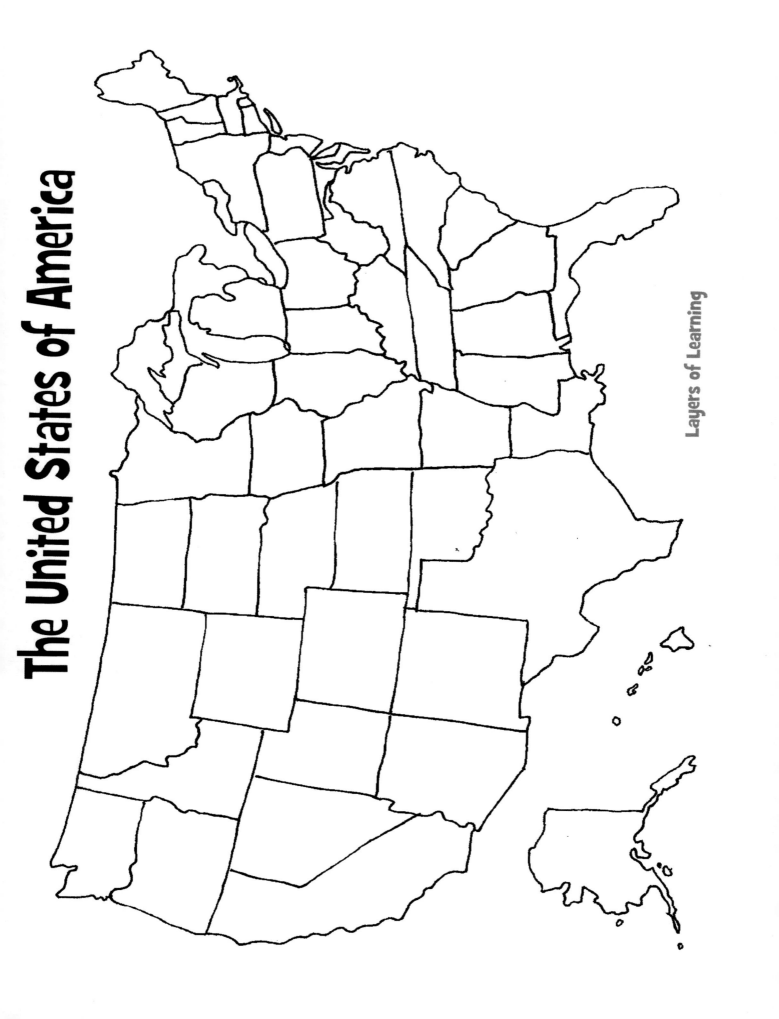

Layers of Learning

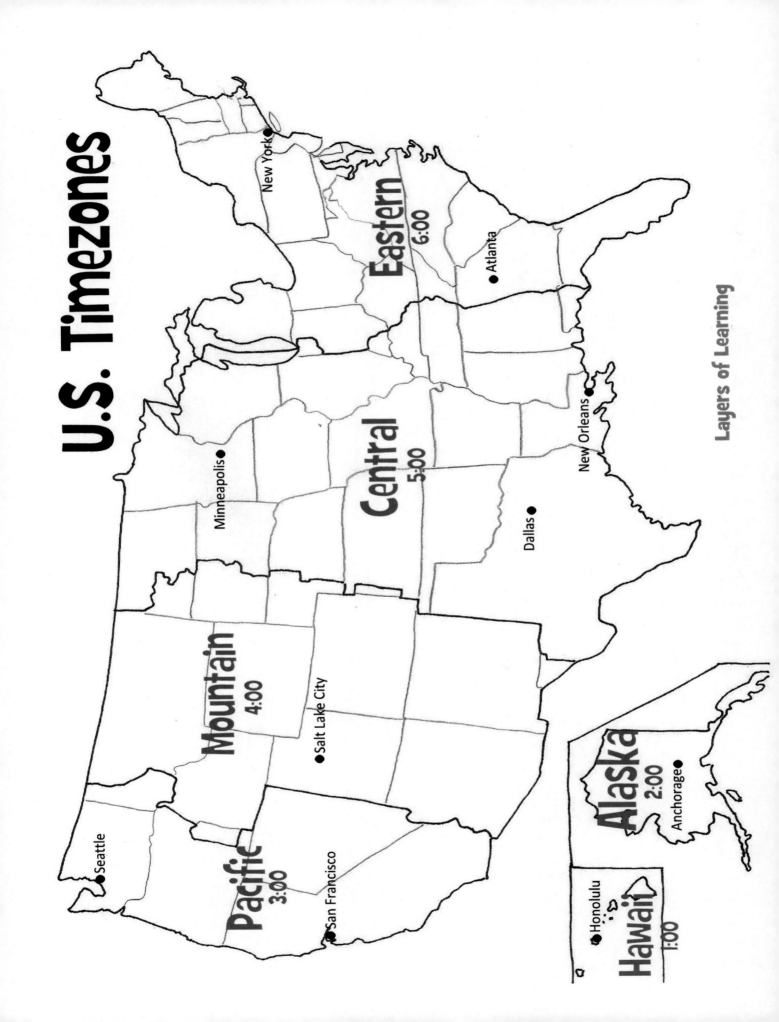

The Star Spangled Banner

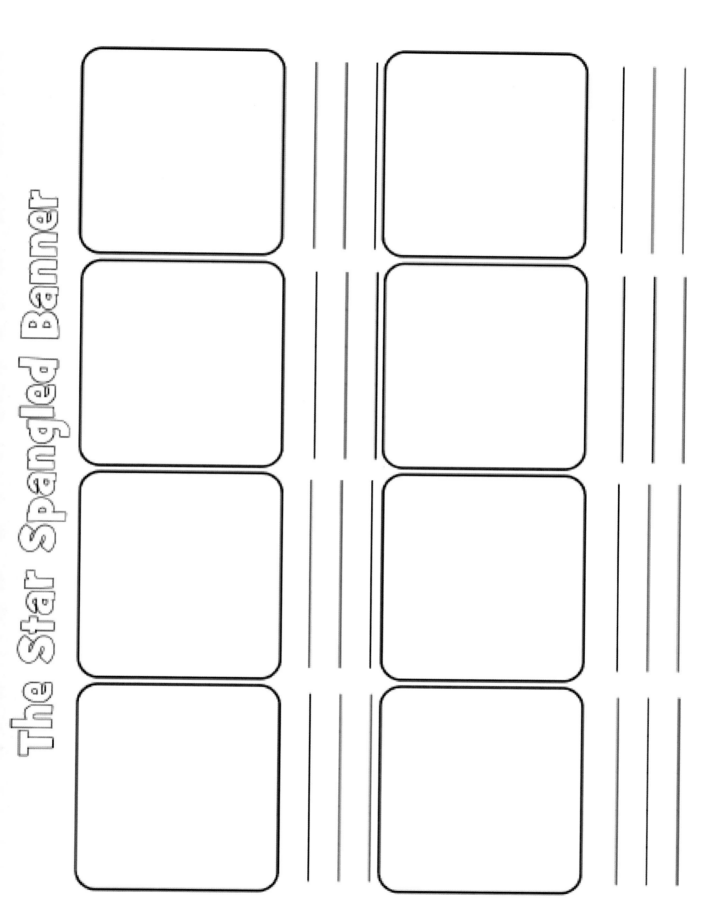

About the Authors

Karen & Michelle . . .
Mothers, sisters, teachers, women who are passionate
about educating kids.
We are dedicated to lifelong learning.

Karen, a mother of four, who has homeschooled her kids for more than eight years with her husband, Bob, has a bachelor's degree in child development with an emphasis in education. She lives in Idaho, gardens, teaches piano, and plays an excruciating number of board games with her kids. Karen is our resident arts expert and English guru {most necessary as Michelle regularly and carelessly mangles the English language and occasionally steps over the bounds of polite society}.

Michelle and her husband, Cameron, have homeschooled their six boys for more than a decade. Michelle earned a bachelors in biology, making her the resident science expert, though she is mocked by her friends for being the Botanist with the Black Thumb of Death. She also is the go-to for history and government. She believes in staying up late, hot chocolate, and a no whining policy. We both pitch in on geography, in case you were wondering.

Visit our constantly updated blog for tons of free ideas,
free printables, and more cool stuff for sale:
www.Layers-of-Learning.com

Made in the USA
Middletown, DE
04 April 2025

73769613R00040